fin(anci)ally free

fin(anci)ally free

11 CONVERSATIONS TO HAVE WITH YOURSELF ABOUT **LIFE, MONEY,** AND **WORTH**

ANDE FRAZIER

ForbesBooks

Published by ForbesBooks, Charleston, South Carolina.
Member of Advantage Media Group.

ForbesBooks is a registered trademark, and the ForbesBooks colophon is a trademark of Forbes Media, LLC.

Printed in the United States of America.

10 9 8 7 6 5 4 3 2 1

ISBN: 978-1-94663-388-0
LCCN: 2019919974

Cover and layout design by David Taylor.

This publication is designed to provide accurate and authoritative information in regard to the subject matter covered. It is sold with the understanding that the publisher is not engaged in rendering legal, accounting, or other professional services. If legal advice or other expert assistance is required, the services of a competent professional person should be sought.

TreeNeutral

Advantage Media Group is proud to be a part of the Tree Neutral® program. Tree Neutral offsets the number of trees consumed in the production and printing of this book by taking proactive steps such as planting trees in direct proportion to the number of trees used to print books. To learn more about Tree Neutral, please visit **www.treeneutral.com**.

Since 1917, the Forbes mission has remained constant. Global Champions of Entrepreneurial Capitalism. ForbesBooks exists to further that aim by bringing the Stories, Passion, and Knowledge of top thought leaders to the forefront. ForbesBooks brings you The Best in Business. To be considered for publication, please visit **www.forbesbooks.com**.

With love always—Sean, Ella, Max, Mom and Dad, Norman, and Vince

Contents

Introduction 1

PART ONE
Core Conversations

Follow the Money: What Your Money Knows about Your Values
and Emotions 7

Make the Shift: Letting Your Personal Values and Goals Guide
Your Money—Not the Other Way Around 25

In Your Corner: Finding the Right Money Mentor 47

Under the Influence: Money Beliefs and Habits You Don't Even
Realize You Picked Up in Childhood 63

All Grown Up: What an Adult Relationship to Money Should
Look Like 75

PART TWO
Conversations to Build Your Worth

Breaking Ground: Four Things That Can Make or Break Your Financial Foundation 89

Feeling Secure: Protecting What You've Built. 103

Love and Money: How Relationships Can Either Solidify or Shatter Your Financial Foundation 121

A New Legacy: Laying the Groundwork for Your Family's Financial Future 133

Expect the Unexpected: Planning for and Predicting the Unpredictable 143

Expect the Expected: Planning for Things You Know Will Happen 153

Conclusion: Your Essential Takeaways. 171

FAQs 175

Resources. 185

About the Author 191

Acknowledgments 193

Introduction

What if I told you that your worth has nothing to do with your bank account, your home value, and the cash you have in your pocket? You would tell me that's obvious, along the same lines as saying, "Money doesn't buy you happiness." But if it were really obvious, then 40 percent of women wouldn't feel overwhelmed when thinking about their finances. Meanwhile, only 9 percent of women report feeling empowered, while 31 percent feel discouraged.[1]

During my more than two decades as a financial strategist, a business leader, an industry recognized speaker, an image consultant, a communications specialist, and a financial life coach, I've worked with hundreds of women across a wide range of situations: Women who were new to the labor force, whether because they were young or returning. Women who were unexpectedly thrust into positions

---

1   Jennifer Brozic, "Nearly 1 in 3 Women in the US Feels Discouraged about Her Finances," Credit Karma, October 4, 2018, https://www.creditkarma.com/insights/i/one-in-three-women-discouraged-finances-survey/.

of financial responsibility, through divorce, death, or even windfalls. Women who changed careers, sold their companies, or quit their jobs on a whim to explore their passions.

Though all these women came to me to discuss financial planning in one sense or another, it was very rare that I ever jumped straight into the mechanics of traditional planning with them. Instead, my approach always began with an understanding of their values and how their personal histories influenced their relationships with money (as a corollary, how those histories influenced their current career or financial situation).

What did these women want out of life? How were their actions moving them toward or away from their goals? Were their decisions grounded in emotion, necessity, reality—or some mix of all three?

The common thread I discovered among these women wasn't that their finances determined their sense of self-worth. In fact, it was the exact opposite: *their sense of self-worth* directly determined their financial situations and decisions.

This made me realize that traditional methods of training women not to tie their worth to money is futile. This is the wrong conversation.

I've since made it my mission to guide women through a process of addressing the ingrained emotions, behaviors, and conditioning that collectively create their sense of self-worth and lead to nonoptimal relationships with money.

In this book, I hope to help you become aware of—and begin reversing—the societal, familial, and personal limitations to financial well-being.

I'll walk you through a number of exercises I've used in thousands of one-on-one sessions over the years and guide you through conversations you must have with yourself to discover what drives your current approach to money.

Instead of giving you one-size-fits-all recommendations, I've designed these conversations to think through different approaches as new financial decisions arise and determine which makes the most sense for you.

We'll explore the emotions that influence your financial decisions and whether these decisions are serving you.

We'll go through what you need to prepare for crisis and the other drains on your financial well-being that divert you from your life goals.

We'll look at where your views on money, finances, and worth originated—and whether the influences from your youth or past should still be relevant today.

You will generate your personal money "maxim" (a short phrase or truth about money that you live by) and have the opportunity to see how that maxim changes as you gain a deeper understanding of your values.

While I tend to err on the side of financial independence, my goal is not to eliminate partners from the picture. A good relationship with money can have a positive impact on your *personal* relationships too. That's because, as you'll discover along the way, money and relationships are often influenced by the same underlying beliefs and values. A lack of trust in relationships, for instance, might also very well manifest in a lack of trust of bosses or other figures that influence your finances.

WHEN IT COMES TO YOUR MONEY, WHAT'S OK?

This is *not* a how-to book. It's not a new series of "thou shalts" and "thou shalt nots." It's a new philosophy—or way of thinking about money and your relationship with it—so that no matter what situation you find yourself in, you have a solid foundation for navigating it.

I want you to reconsider how you think about money and what it says about you. I've set up small, incremental wins to guide and encourage you while you're on the path to larger goals. Give yourself permission to acknowledge every emotion and every concern these conversations bring up.

It's OK to have questions about your money, your values, and your goals.

It's OK not to know where to start.

It's OK to acknowledge the areas where you need more information.

It's OK to not understand why you make the choices, or take the actions, you do around your money and finances.

It is OK to feel overwhelmed at the thought of taking control of your finances and money behavior.

It is OK to realize that not all advice is good advice for you, and not every financial advisor is right for you.

It is OK to realize that previous plans have changed, just as you and your circumstances have likely changed.

It is OK to be resistant about making changes.

You're holding this book. You're ready for some conversations. And that's a good place to start.

—Ande Frazier, CFP®, CLU, ChFC, RICP, BFA™, ChSNC

Featured in *Top 100 People in Finance 2019*

PART ONE

CORE CONVERSATIONS

Money isn't math; it's life.

—Ande Frazier

Follow the Money: What Your Money Knows about Your Values and Emotions

For women, money is less a means of keeping score and more about what it can do, whether offering care for loved ones, enabling pleasures or goals, or salving or burying our hurt feelings. Money, and what it can do, influences our sense of self. Through money, we believe we can demonstrate our desirability, independence, intelligence, power, status, and value.

If you tripped on the word *believe* above, you're already ahead of the game. The next step is understanding the disconnect between what we believe money can do and what it actually does. By creating a well-considered set of goals and values, we can reorient our thinking about the role we want our financial actions to play in our lives.

WHAT DO WOMEN FEEL ABOUT THEIR MONEY?

Over the years, I've listened to women talk about big expenses, whether they are "can't-lose" investments, new house purchases, business opportunities, extravagant vacations, or home remodeling and improvements. They usually talk about what they're doing or how much they're spending. What they don't talk about is how this doing and spending makes them *feel*, even when it makes them feel great. People often get a buzz from exciting investment opportunities or from adding luxuries to their lives.

Whether this euphoria is sustainable is another question. Women who are exploring their true feelings about spending might begin by getting "present" with their emotions. What are they feeling? What are they thinking? What are they doing? After this simple exercise, a wider and deeper range of emotions emerges.

Conversations about paying for private-school education, for instance, can illustrate the range of emotions associated with spending money. People might be delighted at the opportunities school provides. They might have anxiety over a multiyear commitment. They might relish the status that comes with a prestigious institution. They might be concerned that the resulting benefit won't cover the cost. And, depending on where the school is, they might have separation anxiety.

Once women realize a single expenditure can generate a multitude of emotions, they can more easily apply that knowledge to other purchases. A new car may be intended to announce a change in social status. It may represent a realized lifelong aspiration, one that doesn't rely on outside validation. It may come with a change in obligations (such as insurance rates or fuel costs) that prompt a woman to be concerned about her ongoing financial picture. A new car may also inspire guilt: In light of other responsibilities, was it the right decision to make?

Take a new business opportunity: it may be fueled by a desire to be the boss, whether out of revenge for previous bosses' actions or a need to feel empowered. It may be borne from a belief that whatever is being sold will truly benefit the customers. It might be seen as an opportunity to boost one's status or provide one with a sense of self-worth (a primary motivation to launch a business, cited by retirees). Or it may be seen as a path to wealth, which will in turn fund other goals.

WHEN EMOTIONS DRIVE FINANCIAL DECISIONS

It is OK to have strong emotions. But letting them get in the way of sound financial thinking rarely works out well. I knew a partner in an accounting firm who was desperate to leave the stultifying business that didn't satisfy him. He had a gut feeling that a business concept he had toyed with would be an industry disruptor, so he invested his bank accounts and home equity in the idea. The only thing he disrupted was his home life: when his losses mounted, he had no fallback, and his marriage fell apart.

He was out of the accounting firm, but that was about all he accomplished.

Sometimes the trappings of romance and security get in the way of wise financial decisions. Poorly designed prenuptial agreements are one way starry-eyed brides fail to protect themselves. Even well-established brides-to-be can fall into what I call the *successful woman trap.*

A woman who has taken time from a successful career to raise a family may feel her demonstrated earning power allows her to give up financial protections through a prenup. She thinks, *I love my husband-to-be; if anything does go wrong with the marriage, I'll be able to support myself just as I have.*

This is a romantic notion, but it doesn't take into account several realities. First, it will not be easy for her to jump back into the workplace after a multiyear absence. Second, her overall earning potential has been reduced; thus, so has her ability to build a protective financial cushion. And finally, parenthood is full of unforeseen economic costs. Postdivorce is an ugly time to have these realities brought home!

It doesn't take a divorce for emotion-based choices to have disastrous implications. Consider the story of a very-much-in-love couple with three young children. The wife was happily raising her family while her husband was out in the workplace. Their finances were flexible enough to allow for only some of their desires. With their family growing, they opted to finance their "love home," a once-in-a-lifetime property they could grow into and then grow old in. The way they managed to afford it was by skimping on life insurance coverage: they purchased a life insurance policy for the young husband with benefits that wouldn't adequately protect their home investment and provide for the children. He was healthy and in his early thirties.

You already know the story ends tragically. The husband died in an auto accident. The life insurance benefits were barely enough to provide for his widow and their children. And then, shortly after the husband's death, a well-meaning relative hectored the wife into investing the limited amount of insurance money she had received. It went into a real estate scheme "guaranteed to double in value," which would then provide the funds a solid insurance policy would have given her.

In the midst of the wife's emotional chaos, the investment

seemed like a lifeline. It wasn't. She ended up moving in with her parents. Her father, who had planned to retire, kept working to support a family of five. Her mother, who had been looking forward to a life of leisure, was tasked with helping raise three grandchildren while her daughter worked.

While this story may seem soap-opera tragic, it's not. It's an emotions-driven scenario I've encountered (with varying details, of course) more times than I would have imagined.

EMOTIONS AND YOUR FINANCES

When it comes to your finances, there are no right or wrong ways to feel. The first step here is to acknowledge *all* the emotions tied to money and financial activity. The step following that one is to acknowledge how an expenditure fulfills, or does not fulfill, one's desires.

Most financial decisions larger than buying a cup of coffee are life decisions, which benefit from being evaluated clearheadedly. But even people who can make a finance-based argument for their actions are missing the key consideration of their emotions.

We'll go through some emotion-based exercises, but don't just rely on this book (or any book). When you use any financial advisor, note whether he or she asks about how your feelings are influencing your choices. Without taking the time to "get present" with emotions, anyone can make an ill-fated decision, or, conversely, miss out on a genuinely worthwhile opportunity due to fear of the unknown.

If you think this sounds like a psychological approach to financial decisions, you're correct. Humans are masters at finding great-sounding reasons for doing ill-considered things. As science fiction author Robert A. Heinlein once wrote, "Man is not a rational animal; he is a rationalizing animal."

What's more, emotion-based actions go beyond large financial decisions, to even the smallest and most immediate. Retailers know that. Look at the steps they take to transfer more of your money seamlessly to their pockets. Preordering and pickup, phone-based payment, and one-click purchasing all have one element in common: they remove pauses that allow consumers to take the time to logically consider their purchases.

Every time a consumer reaches for a wallet, or into a pocket or purse, it creates a barrier to a sale, and those who hawk products or services know how to eliminate those barriers. Removing those barriers is easy today because most people have their phones in hand or conveniently nearby. Ordering that extra coffee, taxi ride, or additional product just gets smoother and smoother. Endless daily purchases can now be automatic and unthinking. Impulses rule.

Don't get me wrong. I love Amazon. The massive range of goods, the usually decent prices, and reliable delivery have made it both useful and fun. But at the same time, if I'm not able to see my actual bank balance decrease as I spend (there's a difference between viewing an e-receipt and monitoring a diminishing bank balance) or feel my wallet get lighter as I spend cash, there is less of an opportunity to consider my purchase and get present with my emotions.

Retailers profit when you don't think. I'm not saying don't have coffee, but I am saying take the time to thoughtfully consider the decision, rather than have it be the unthinking purchase your favorite coffee-shop-with-app or online retailer loves. Do you want that second daily barista coffee at $4.50 per? Or do you need that $22.50 a week ($95 a month and $1,140 a year) to go toward your island vacation?

And before anyone thinks I'm some sort of martyr—yes, I consciously decide that I must have that second cup of coffee.

Step One: Identifying Your Money-Based Emotions

There's a difference between buying a cup of coffee and making a big-ticket purchase. To help identify your emotional reaction to spending, imagine receiving a $10,000 gift (not an inheritance; you want something with as few emotional strings as possible). What is your unvarnished, gut-level reaction to each of the following possible uses? If avoiding writing them down, or writing them on a separate piece of paper, will give you the freedom to be honest with yourself, please do so.

1. This is free money, and I'm spending it on indulgences and luxuries.

2. I want to create once-in-a-lifetime memories, such as through travel.

3. I didn't earn this money, so I'm donating it to my favorite charity.

4. I am going to deposit this money and access it only when I have a real need for it.

5. This is additional cash I can put toward paying monthly bills and other financial obligations.

6. My retirement cushion just got a little more padding.

7. I will use this money to help pay for my children's or grandchildren's education.

8. I will ask someone with more experience than I have what I should do with it.

9. I will look for an opportunity to double this money through investment.

10. I now have a down payment on a major expense (e.g., car, time-share, home improvement).

11. I am a pretty good money manager. I'll incorporate the money into my portfolio.

12. I'm going to pay down some of my larger debts.

13. Other scenarios not listed.

Once you have considered each of your emotional responses to the scenarios, look for groups of similar emotions. Which ones make you feel as though you are denying yourself? Which ones give you validation? Which ones give you pleasure? Which ones make you angry?

There are no correct or incorrect answers. There are only insights into how various behaviors make you feel—and whether these actions have an impact on your financial decisions.

The money-based emotions exercise should give you a baseline sense of how certain financial activities might make you feel. As you consider your values and goals, that baseline may change. In fact, unless you've already spent a lot of time thinking about your "worth"—not just your financial worth, but what validates you as well—the baseline probably *will* change.

WOMEN'S VALUES MATTER

Beyond worth, there are values and a basic philosophy of finances that help determine someone's emotional approach to money. These values, like education, environment, and experience, aren't set in stone but actually change throughout someone's life.

Geography, religion, and economic circumstances can all influence how a woman sees herself. Available wealth, of course, is key. Families that experience boom-and-bust cycles are more likely to produce children who think financial circumstances will sort themselves out, while those coming from modest steady income streams have a better chance of being raised with a stronger sense of budgeting.

When parenting responsibilities are not evenly shared, women usually take on larger nonpaying roles. They also are more likely to serve as caregivers to both their own and their husbands' parents. In short, partly because of how they are raised, women often take on roles and responsibilities that differ from men's. As a result, their values differ too. They tend to favor stability and security over financial gain.

Women are also more likely to consider how their own incapacitation might affect their ability to care for their loved ones or even themselves. For instance, although many long-term-care financial products cost more for women than they do for men, women account for 70–80 percent of long-term-care insurance claims.[2] And since women are living longer than men and often find themselves living alone, they are less likely to have a family member who can serve as a caregiver; therefore, they have a greater need for financial resources to cover the cost of long-term-care facilities.[3]

---

2   Sarah Stevenson, "Paying for Senior Care: Women vs. Insurance," *Senior Living Blog*, A Place for Mom, June 13, 2019, https://www.aplaceformom.com/blog/2013-3-26-women-and-long-term-care-insurance/.

3   "A Woman's Guide to Long-Term Care," American Council of Life Insurers, accessed November 12, 2019, https://www.acli.com/Consumer-Info/Long-Term-Care-Insurance/LTC-For-Women.

Advisors Who Care about Women's Values

A financial advisor who has worked with a number of female clients is more likely to consider a woman's income, debt, retirement plans, and savings and assets, as well as other financial concerns. And a really good advisor will also consider a woman's *life* status: whether she has children, has living parents, or has other potential dependents, including potential medical costs. In short, that advisor will provide contingencies for the influences that may mean the difference between a stable life and a scrambling one.

An advisor may also recognize a woman who is disposed toward sacrificing her present for future potential needs. A *good* advisor will structure programs that allow a female client to balance her future-based aspirations, dreams, and concerns against an unsatisfying present life.

The more a woman has considered her values and goals, the better she'll be able to give her advisor the details necessary to create a program that meets current needs and desires in addition to future concerns. The best financial advisors also realize that some activities or purchases are best enjoyed earlier in life and will build in opportunities for these activities, even if it means the overall value of the portfolio the advisor manages shrinks.

How Women's Values Are Changing

I mentioned environmental influences on values. Changes to retail culture mentioned previously (such as cashless, even wallet-less transactions), along with the increasing ubiquity of "buy it now" and one-day delivery options, have done more than make purchasing frictionless. Today's youngest adult consumers have grown up in a world in which these features have always been present, and their thoughts about finances reflect their world.

As they have joined adulthood, language has changed to reflect their relationship with money. Younger consumers have embraced YOLO (you only live once) and FOMO (fear of missing out) as linguistic shortcuts that reflect the normalization of impulse purchases.

The "spend now, live now" approach has resulted in millennials (loosely defined as people born between 1982 and 2000) having among the lowest personal savings rates of any generation. Financial planning and long-term strategizing were alien concepts to them: most held off planning home purchases, families, and even car purchases until later in life than their older siblings, parents, and grandparents did.

This generation's fear of missing out has led its members to job hop more than others. They believe that if they are able to augment their titles and increase their responsibilities, they may bring home higher salaries. But this activity also curtails their ability to start contributing to retirement accounts and prevents them from becoming fully vested in them, thereby taking advantage of employer matching funds.

Do millennials care? They didn't initially. But as they have aged (in 2019, the oldest millennials hit their late thirties), they are finally embracing the job stability necessary for marriages and starting families.

Millennials have access to more readily available financial information than any previous generation. Unfortunately, it's taken them some time to realize they can't spend all they have today and expect life to work out tomorrow. Fortunately, even those who are just now starting to explore their psychological and philosophical approaches to finances will be able to modify financial behaviors and thus improve their lives.

ARE YOU LIKE SALLY?

Meet Sally, a composite of women in their thirties who make a decent salary, have settled into a career, yet are new to the idea of financial planning.

Sally is single. She has worked hard but never seems to get ahead financially or even reduce her debt. For our Sally example, the reason is clear: Sally has treated shopping as a form of consolation or self-medication. Here's how it's worked: Something in Sally's life would trigger feelings of insecurity or anxiety. Then, to make herself feel better, she would browse online and buy something special—maybe a handbag, jewelry, or a new outfit.

As a human resources director, Sally was exposed to a constant stream of professional women dressed to impress. Some worked at her company; others were seeking jobs there. Sally couldn't help herself from feeling that she deserved what these other women had. If, after working steadily for a decade and a half, she couldn't have items of similar value, she'd be missing out!

What Sally *didn't* know is how these other women had financed their goodies. All she knew was that after each purchase she made, she'd experience guilt and anger about what she had bought. Then her sense of self-worth would plummet. The emotions Sally experienced were nowhere near the joy and self-assurance she had been hoping to feel in her new clothes.

That wasn't all. When Sally saw other people achieving high-ticket financial goals—travel, home ownership, continuing education programs, substantial charitable donations—the sense of worth she had sought through her purchases felt even further away.

"I'm not even able to save money like other people," Sally (just as other women like her) would lament. But she faced a larger question.

Money was only a *thing*, similar to the apparel she bought without thinking. How could money, too, cause her such emotional distress?

THE ROAD TO CONTROL

We'll follow Sally through her self-discovery. I'll promise a happy ending in advance: while we won't take her through the elimination of all her debt, we'll see how she took control of her finances through embracing patience and consistency, two behaviors she would nurture. Importantly, even before she modified any of her behavior, Sally began to see that women's values do matter! She then explored her *true* values and goals. Her unique goals would become the most powerful motivators she could have had.

We'll return to Sally in upcoming conversations. But we can use her initial avoidance of financial planning to illustrate a larger point. For many women, financial planning is something that happens passively, as opposed to something they actively engage in. A woman is more likely to give philanthropic work priority over her personal financial situation and education. Doing so may contribute to her sense of self-worth, but it comes at the expense of her self-preservation.

When faced with the need to take control of money, women often become immobilized. "I can't deal with this right now" is a common refrain. Sometimes a woman will surrender control to someone who doesn't have her best interests at heart (an individual motivated by malice or simply unconcerned with her interests). Then, once responsibility for the financial crisis has passed, the need to go back and calmly take control gets pushed to the bottom of the pile, further removing her from action.

That's why, when a woman needs to exert financial responsibility,

I suggest she think of it as "response-*ability*"; the ability to respond to a crisis in a clear and thoughtful manner that will ameliorate the crisis and eventually serve both her short- and long-term goals. There are steps that allow a woman to achieve such response-ability, but the foundation for those steps needs to be in place *before* a crisis hits.

How Well Are You Prepared to Meet a Financial Crisis?

The earlier investigation into identifying your money-based emotions didn't require you to write anything down. This checklist offers useful indicators regarding how crisis ready you are. The points offer a start for providing emotionally, financially, and physically for you and your loved ones. For now, scan the list below to get a general sense of where you are in your ability to take charge of a crisis. And of course, feel free to checkmark the ones you achieve!

- **I have interviewed, chosen, and worked with a financial advisor** trained in areas of importance to me (women's issues, retirement planning, diversified investing advice, etc.).

- **I have learned to identify my money-related emotions, values, and goals** and clearheadedly move through financial decision-making processes to keep my stated values and goals aligned.

- **I have added relevant advisors to my financial team as appropriate:** estate attorney, accountant, independent insurance professional, and so on.

- **With professional assistance, I have finalized essential paperwork:** will or trust, living will, power of attorney, healthcare directive, and so on and have put all necessary forms of insurance in place: life, health, long-term care, home, and auto.

- **I have informed relevant family members of the people on my financial team, including full contact information.**

- **I have informed relevant family members of the whereabouts of important financial, insurance, and estate planning documents** and have included locations of safe-deposit boxes and keys. All bank signatories are in place to allow access to safe-deposit boxes.

- **I have created a list of all relevant banks, financial institutions, insurance companies, and pension funds** (and their account or policy numbers) and the approximate value of the assets within each (as of a specific date). I have set reminders to regularly update the corresponding values and update any institutional changes or additions as they happen.

- **I have written personal letters or notes for family members designed to help avoid conflict or misunderstandings.** These letters clearly communicate my end-of-life wishes and important thoughts regarding my loved ones; they also detail which special items I intended to leave to which family members.

- **I have informed all relevant family members of the whereabouts of essential passwords** to critical websites such as those related to insurance policies, long-term care, and so on. I have also included all current passwords they might need for utilities, essential service providers, home care, healthcare professionals, and others. I have kept my password records up to date.

- **I have shared with all relevant family members the location of all essential keys** and digital pass codes for my house, garage, storage, and other important places.

- **I have shared with all relevant family members a full listing of important neighbors or others** who might be of assistance to them.

FINANCIAL PLANNING DESIGNED FOR WOMEN, NOT MEN

There's no need to jump up and start assembling all the items listed above. We'll go through some exercises first that will help you to shop for the best action plan to facilitate your goals. For now, the most important concept is this: *most financial information has traditionally been designed for men.* But while men's primary financial goal may be the pursuit of profit, myWorth (www.myworthfinance.com) research has revealed that *women primarily value financial security.*

These aren't absolutes, and it is perfectly reasonable for men and women to want different things, but their financial choices should be conscious. They should not be predetermined by the available programs and materials, which may have been designed to appeal to men.

This does not mean women are more risk averse than men. There's a difference between avoiding risk and finding strategies that ensure women are safe, secure, and protected from future harm.

Within this, the *level* of risk can vary.

The problem is that, even if a woman is left money after her male partner dies, she may have trouble finding the advice that is right for her. Financial advisors often don't change their strategies for the female left behind. As a result, the strategies offered by the original family advisor become less relevant. The opportunity to take control of the finances and have them contribute to a *woman's* sense of worth is never addressed.

For all the women trying (in vain) to fit into traditional men's-size financial shoes—and for all the Sallys of the world—here's what I'd like to leave you with for now: *the power of money does not have to be something everybody else has.* Our next conversation explores the values, goals, and behaviors that will enrich your life, both financially and—just as importantly—in nonmonetary worth. Exploring this question will also establish a terrific foundation for finding your best possible financial advocate.

Make the Shift: Letting Your Personal Values and Goals Guide Your Money— Not the Other Way Around

When feminist Gloria Steinem wrote, "We can tell our values by looking at our checkbook stubs," she was only half right. What checkbook stubs (or e-statements, in today's world) indicate is women's behavior and the values that behavior reflect. Women who haven't considered their core values often don't make purchases based on what they want in life. Altering the spending behaviors that rob women of the life they desire must start with a clear-eyed assessment of core values. Consider people who unwittingly live their lives according to the values their parents, spouses, or partners choose to live by. You may have heard a friend say, "I *should* be saving for a bigger condo," "I *should* be investing more than I am," or "I *shouldn't* plan this vacation; it's too self-indulgent."

And yet her behaviors don't align with those "I should" statements, because the statements don't reflect her core values. Clarifying values is the first step before asking the essential questions: "What goals will fulfill or align with my values?" and "Which behaviors will get me to those goals?"

WHEN VALUES AND GOALS ARE OUT OF ALIGNMENT

For Sally, the thirty-something from the previous chapter who was exploring her values and worth, ongoing purchases of expensive apparel and accessories might indicate she was materialistic and pre-occupied with appearance. But those were her *money* behaviors. Such behaviors can be greatly influenced by emotions. Sally's *core* values might not be represented by her spending behaviors at all.

Sally's values (what she thought she should be doing with her money) and her goals (what would actually bring her long-term satisfaction) were misaligned. Sally struggled to reconcile her personal values regarding money with the value she had been raised with: money is the root of all evil; people shouldn't use it for personal gain or enjoyment; and above all, people don't *ever* talk about it, even when they need financial counseling.

These values had permeated her life. Although grown-up Sally didn't actually embrace those beliefs, she hadn't been willing to let her childhood values go.

According to Sally's childhood beliefs, having money to spend meant she was selfish. For Sally, the things she said she aspired to— her personal goals, hopes, and dreams—were things that represented selflessness. She had trouble discussing anything self-indulgent. To Sally, aspirational ideas, which would provide her material pleasure or comfort, represented avarice and self-absorption. But her actions, her behavior, her "checkbook stubs" reflected different values.

LIVING A MONEY MAXIM

To find her real values, Sally did an exercise that helped her determine her "money maxim"—that personal truth we referred to earlier. She did an exercise in which she thought about money and then completed the phrases "When it comes to money, I am _____, and I am not _____." The exercise Sally completed is an essential first step for anybody seeking to uncover and change her relationship toward finances. Figuring out your money maxim, and therefore your emotional relationships with money, starts with an honest conversation with yourself. What follows is a guided exercise that will make the conversation easier.

What's Your Secret Money Maxim?

To uncover your emotional relationship to money, as opposed to the money mindset you assumed was operational for you, do the following:

1. At the top of a piece of paper, fill in your answers to the two blanks in the following sentences. Since you are the only person who will see these, give yourself permission to honestly record your thoughts: "When it comes to money, I am _____; I am not _____." Examples: "When it comes to money, I am impatient; I am not deliberative." Or, "When it comes to money, I am willing to spend on others; I am not comfortable buying things for myself."

2. Next, divide the space below this first two-sentence money maxim into three columns. In the left-hand column, list the expenditures and their costs from the past month that were *outside* your monthly operating budget. That is, those outside rent, utilities, food, gas, medicine, and anything else you might have budgeted for ahead of time. These might include unplanned family expenses; social events such as birthdays, drinks, or meals out; spur-of-the-moment apparel or health and beauty purchases; loans or outright gifts; replenishing household items you hadn't realized were running out; new household items; or anything else for which you hadn't mentally or physically put money aside.

3. In the middle column, list the positive and negative feelings and thoughts you experienced before and during the expenditure to the left. Don't be afraid to express selfish or unpopular sentiments: this list is for *you*. Examples: "Felt insecure about an upcoming event; wanted to look as attractive as my friends," "Was excited about buying that new leather jacket," "Avoided thinking about not being able to afford a weekend trip, so put it on a charge card to deal with later," or "Felt good about purchase because it would get me closer to my budgeted goal of _____."

4. In the right-hand column, describe your feelings after the purchase or event for which it was acquired. Examples: "Felt guilty," "Worth it," "Knew I didn't deserve it," "Was proud of myself for finally making the expenditure," or "Felt entitled."

5. Read over your middle- and right-hand column thoughts and feelings and note recurring emotional patterns. Then fill in the two blanks, this time keeping your *new* feelings in mind: "When it comes to money, I am _____; I am not _____." There are no right or wrong answers. You may even list several money maxims initially, but eventually there will be one that stands out—that clicks and feels true. When that happens, that is when you know you have found your true money maxim. The one that rules all the others.

6. This exercise enables you to get in touch with your genuine feelings about your money maxim. Doing so is the first step in figuring out financial goals that take into account your persistent emotions about money. In the next step, you'll determine your core values and align your emotions with them.

Sally's responses to this exercise were telling. Her initial feelings about money yielded a money maxim many women hold: "I am inadequate; I am not worthy." Sally was spending her life alternately trying to prove she was worthy of having money and nice things and then combatting her childhood programming: the desire to have nice things undercut her worth as a person.

What's more, a money maxim such as "I am inadequate; I am not worthy" often extends to aspects of life beyond the financial. This exercise can reveal just how intertwined our lives, our money, and our emotions really are.

Sally's next step was creating a new money mantra. Where her initial maxim had been all about financial deprivation and scarcity, her new mantra was the opposite: "I am worthy of abundance and financial affluency."

Sally's new mantra set her on a path to building the financial security she desired. Creating the mantra, however, was only the first step. To help her internalize it, she jotted it on index cards and placed it around her home and office. She also put a card with her mantra written on it in her wallet—near her credit cards.

Sally's mantra consistently reassured her that accumulating and saving money for her goals were valid life actions, and she was entitled to that abundancy as long as she worked to achieved it.

BEHAVIOR CHANGE STARTS WITH VALUES

Sally then reconciled her money mantra (which represented her underlying *attitude* toward money) with her actions. When she reviewed her spending behavior, she realized it was making her miserable. She would purchase expensive apparel in an effort to alter people's perception of her. She wanted to demonstrate she was doing well and was worthy of nice things.

In truth, her spending made her feel even worse. The emotions she listed next to each purchase did not reflect a healthy relationship with spending. Sally's purchases had little to do with her genuine needs, plans, or goals. Her spending was all about how it made Sally feel *at that instant.*

When she looked at her bills and realized she wouldn't be able to pay them, she felt far, far worse.

Sally's spending behavior made her so miserable that it clearly wasn't in line with her core values. Her next step was determining what those values were through the following exercise:

Uncover Your Five Core Values

First, review the list below and cross out any items not germane to your core values.

1. Achievement
2. Advancement
3. Adventure
4. Authority
5. Being There for Others
6. Building Things
7. Challenging Problems
8. Change and Variety
9. Close Relationships
10. Communication
11. Community
12. Competence
13. Competition
14. Connection
15. Cooperation
16. Creativity
17. Decency
18. Decisiveness
19. Democracy
20. Economic Security
21. Effectiveness
22. Enjoying Life
23. Ethical Practice
24. Excellence
25. Excitement
26. Expertise
27. Faith
28. Fame
29. Family
30. Financial Gain
31. Freedom
32. Friendships
33. Growth
34. Health and Well-Being
35. Helping Others
36. Honesty
37. Humor
38. Independence
39. Influencing Others
40. Integrity
41. Involvement
42. Joy
43. Kindness
44. Leadership
45. Love
46. Loyalty
47. Making a Difference in the World
48. Market Position
49. Meaningful Work
50. Money Knowledge
51. Nature
52. Openness
53. Order

54. Peace
55. Persistence
56. Personal Development
57. Physical Challenge
58. Pleasure
59. Power
60. Pride
61. Privacy
62. Profit
63. Promotion
64. Public Service
65. Quality Relationships
66. Recognition
67. Religion
68. Security
69. Selflessness
70. Self-Motivation
71. Self-Realization
72. Self-Respect
73. Serenity
74. Service
75. Society
76. Spending Time with Others
77. Spiritual Beliefs
78. Stability
79. Status
80. Supervising Others
81. Teaching
82. Teamwork
83. Time
84. Truth
85. Wealth
86. Winning
87. Wisdom
88. Working with Others
89. Working Alone
90. Working under Pressure

Second, eliminate entries you feel duplicate others. Retain the one most pertinent to your life. For example, if Religion, Faith, and Spiritual Beliefs mean the same thing to you, keep the one that resonates most strongly.

Third, choose between twelve and fifteen items from the remaining list.

Finally, choose the five values that represent what is most important to you. Eliminate values by asking yourself, *Could I live my life without this value?*

Sally quickly picked fifteen important values. When she had to narrow it down even more, she wavered between those truly hers and those based on societal mores or her family upbringing.

She made her final cuts by determining whether she was considering a specific value because she thought it would make her worthy in someone else's eyes. Once she applied that to her choices, she easily rejected values that weren't hers. She chose the following:

Independence—Not surprising, given the tug-of-war between what she wanted to do and what she was raised to do. Independence was a breakthrough value for Sally.

Community—Sally had been raised with community as a core value, and she happily embraced it. Community meant family and opportunities for contributions that made Sally feel good about herself.

Security—Though Sally wanted to be independent, she also wanted to feel secure through personal success. Additionally, financial security would enable Sally's independence value.

Recognition—Sally wanted her work within her community and profession acknowledged. Her parents instilled in her a strong sense of duty, and she wished to make her own mark. She felt that if the value of her work were recognized, she would no longer rely on personal acquisitions for validation.

Spiritual Beliefs—Sally believed in service to God and gained joy from being active in her church.

Sally's next step was determining the wealth requirement she would need to realize these five goals. Her desire to be secure meant making sure she had enough money to survive for six months without worrying about additional income. In addition to security, that cushion would also give her independence. She would not need outside help or loans if she lost her job. Furthermore, Sally enjoyed being a single woman and wanted to make sure she could retain that independent status, if she chose.

ARE YOUR GOALS ALIGNED?

Once you have identified your core values, you can design financial goals that reflect these values. Honesty and candor are critical. There is often a split between people's stated goals and their behaviors. They may express noble thoughts, but their financial actions tell another story. For instance, people claim providing for their family is a core value, yet they fail to have the following:

- Adequate savings to protect the family

- Life, disability, and long-term-care insurance

- A living will, health directives, testamentary will, or estate planning

- A plan to help fund college

- Easily accessible information regarding bank accounts, legal documents, and financial statements

What *do* these folks have in abundance? Misguided sentiments such as, "I'll figure that out later. I've got time to handle that." The essential question is, Are your *actions* in line with your true values? Here's how Sally oriented her actions to goals that reflected her five chosen values:

Independence and Security—All along, Sally had wanted to get rid of her debt. But without understanding how that goal related to her core values, she was going to have trouble doing so. In fact, she was plunging deeper into debt without understanding why her payoff goal was so elusive. All she knew was that being debt-free would mean she wouldn't "feel bad all the time."

By examining the underlying purpose of being debt-free, Sally saw how essential independence and security were to *who she is* and how the burdens of debt made living these values impossible.

Knowing this inspired her to stay on track, as she could then weigh which purchases she could live without to make her chosen values a reality.

Before Sally could become debt-free, she needed to learn about *bad* debt versus *good* debt. The purchases she made to assuage her anxiety and feelings of inadequacy, which she charged on high-interest credit cards, represented bad, strangulating debt.

But Sally also learned about good debt: planned, affordable, and sometimes deductible purchases made today that would benefit her for months or years to come. If she chose to purchase her own home, she could take a greater role in her personal security. She would also have the financial security of not being beholden to a landlord or the fluctuations of the real estate market. When it came to bad debt versus good debt, Sally began to see that some financial obligations could be tools that enabled present goals.

In the meantime, to achieve her core goals of independence and security, Sally needed to eliminate all bad, unproductive debt in the form of her credit card bills. She worked with a financial advocate to devise a self-motivating plan that would eliminate her debt without making her resent what she had to give up.

Community, Spiritual Beliefs—Sally wanted to consistently tithe 10 percent of her income to her church. She hoped to do this without falling deeper into debt or otherwise limiting herself.

Recognition—Leaving a legacy to her community both fulfilled Sally's desire to assist others and provided affirmation of genuine worthiness in Sally's (and others') eyes. That recognition was one of her key core values.

BALANCING TOMORROW'S GOALS WITH TODAY'S

Like many people, Sally's core values were intertwined. But before she could devise a plan to help her achieve her future goals, she needed to balance those goals with her life in the present. Realizing part of our goals in the present through small early wins helps power ourselves toward future objectives.

Sally sought to balance between having immediate enjoyment while working toward her value-driven goals. As part of her Community value, she wanted to leave something meaningful as a bequest, such as a significant donation to a local school or hospital or a scholarship for underprivileged youths. Doing so would also give her a sense of recognition (another of her top five values), thereby achieving an additional goal.

Sally could certainly set up financial plans to ensure the legacy would be in place. But she also needed to enjoy contributing to her community in the present day in a manner that would help her experience a level of recognition in the present. The challenge was making a contribution that wouldn't impinge on future giving.

The solution was volunteering. Sally already taught Sunday school in her church, but she had loved being a cheerleader when she was in high school and always wished she could impart the skill to youngsters. It wouldn't cost her anything to offer her services to the town recreation center.

Sally pitched her idea of cheerleading for fun, not competition, to a recreation center administrator who thought it was a wonderful idea. The center was always looking for new youth programs. Sally's class quickly grew from five girls to twenty. Sally loved bringing excitement and challenge into her students' lives, enjoyed the community recognition her volunteer work brought her, and later confided, "I've never experienced this much pure joy!"

Having achieved an immediate level of recognition and satisfaction, she was able to focus on her longer-term giving back to the community. And the stores where she had been spending money without gaining joy survived without her.

ACTION PLANS THAT WORK

Achieving both "tomorrow" and "today" goals means first aligning values with goals, then creating plans necessary to meet those goals. In some cases, plotting present-day actions can seem as challenging as crafting future plans!

Not knowing how to go about doing something is often the very thing that keeps people from their dreams. They tell themselves, "I'm never going to get there," and so they don't begin.

A visual stimulation can jump-start the process. Sally moved from being daunted by her goals to being inspired by them by creating a vision-board collage of what achieving those goals might look like. As she worked on her collage, she realized she could do the following:

- Find pictures that represented how she would feel (free and strong) once she had accumulated the six months of living expenses in savings

- Cut and paste photos of travel destinations, home settings, and zero-balance credit card statements, reminding her of what financial independence would look like

- Add a faux newspaper story about the legacy she would leave to her community, including details about the people who would benefit from it

What makes a vision board effective is unearthing your own values and goals, depicting them, and setting up an action plan. In doing so, you don't avoid feeling like you're heading to the grocery store with someone else's shopping list. You've embraced *your* values and chosen *your own* goals. You are not taking action with a sense of obligation; you are selecting a powerful route to goals and actions that you are excited about.

Creating a vision board is not a one-and-done proposition. Just as financial planning has to be periodically updated to reflect changing circumstances, vision boards should be updated to reflect new goals and achieved goals—and to continue keeping you involved and in touch with your goals.

Being excited and *staying* excited is essential. While action steps for present or future goals may be baby steps, they need to be followed consistently and often—daily, weekly, or at least monthly.

SMALL CONSISTENT STEPS

Sally's future goals of security and independence were not likely to be fulfilled unless she eliminated her spiraling credit card debt, refrained from adding new bad debt, and created the six-month repository of living expenses that she wanted as a cushion for job changing and unexpected life events. (These living expenses should be in an accessible account separate from a checking account.) The key to Sally's security and independence was an action plan of small consistent steps that would do the following:

- **Reduce the financial uncertainty of large steps through "chunking."** Taking frequent action enables incremental victories. Additionally, small consistent steps don't feel like huge commitments, even if they are building toward a large one! The prospect of saving six months of living expenses seemed overwhelming to Sally at first. But she plotted out and saved a week's worth of savings and then moved her goal to two weeks. Because Sally was saving toward an incremental goal, it was easy for her to track and appreciate those small successes quickly.

She applied the same graduated chunking approach to tithing. Though she had wanted to earmark 10 percent of her annual income for year-round donating to her church, she approached that goal gently, first tithing at 4 percent, then 6 percent, and then 8 percent. Each time, the actions she took were small enough not to have a huge impact on her lifestyle, but she still was being recognized for her contributions. By the time she got to 10 percent, she was already enjoying her sense of achievement.

- **Change habits and rewire the brain.** The most effective way of changing habits is by taking small consistent actions that are easy to perform and consistently reward or reinforce your core values. Eventually those actions become instinctive habits because the brain has rewired itself to respond to them in a particular manner. In some cases, the brain misses those actions if you skip or stop them: these actions have become pleasures!

- **Automate certain actions to eliminate possibility of self-sabotage or neglect.** Automating payment, savings, charitable giving, and transfer actions through your bank or vendors is easy. Automating can prove helpful to individuals who often forget or are too busy to attend to their accounts or who might need a way to help them avoid indulging in spontaneous spending.

- **Allow conscious consideration of financial activities to consistently reaffirm goals.** Whether Sally's transfers to savings were automated or not, she wanted to make sure she acknowledged, "I'm making this decision because I need security, and I'd rather not have a new phone or designer shoes so I can build toward six months of financial security that will support my independence." Being conscious about money transfers and purchases requires people to consistently reaffirm, "I'm doing this, and this is why."

> By keeping values and goals up front, it becomes more difficult to ignore them and enable undesired behavior such as making frivolous, unbudgeted, or ultimately unsatisfying purchases.

By keeping values and goals up front, it becomes more difficult to ignore them and enable undesired behavior such as making frivolous, unbudgeted, or ultimately unsatisfying purchases.

Without consistent reaffirmation, people run the risk of losing the connection to the core values they worked to establish.

- **Build a sense of accomplishment quickly.** Sally knew money is closely linked to emotions; she was concerned her emotions would affect her ability to follow her action plan. Consider her desire to pay down her debt. A conventional financial pro would have advised, "Pay down the credit card with either the highest interest rate or highest balance first." On paper, those approaches are logical. Higher interest rates make a balance more expensive to maintain. And a higher balance with a lower rate generates more finance charges over the longer time needed to reduce it, especially if a consumer is paying only the minimum.

Either payment tactic *seems* logical. Yet neither method would be the best approach if Sally became discouraged during the pay-down process and abandoned or reduced her efforts to eliminate her debt. Sally knew that gaining a quick sense of accomplishment would be the best way for her to stay excited about her debt-elimination goals.

So, she went for the credit card with the lowest balance, the one easiest to pay off. Sally wanted the thrill of a real accomplishment: eliminating a debt as quickly as possible. Rather than spread her debt-elimination funds evenly across her six credit cards, she paid the minimum on every card except the one with the lowest balance. That card got the rest of her money. Sally paid off her lowest-balance card in under three months and was elated. Then she used the same technique to keep moving forward with successes.

The sense of accomplishment she gained was far more valuable to her than the cost of the extra interest on her other cards. Her small but significant victory strengthened her resolve to stay with the program and pay off her debt.

Sally's action plan for achieving independence and security also included measures that didn't involve money. Because she didn't have a partner, she needed to put her advance directives, her healthcare proxy and living will, and other long-term and estate planning efforts in place. Her early successes paying down her debt and building six months of savings benefitted her peace of mind and gave her the confidence she needed to tackle retirement goals.

ONGOING BEHAVIOR MODIFICATION: STOP, BREATHE, FEEL

When events crop up that go against a woman's core values and personal goals, old spending behaviors may resurface.

Dealing with these instances is easier in some cases than others. It's easy to say, "Whoa—that new sports car is not in the plan! I can't do that!" But aligning values, goals, and behavior across changing life stages is trickier. What if values, and thus goals, have genuinely morphed as years pass? A twenty-year-old woman might have a core value of spiritual growth and exploration. At thirty, she might have earned more money than she dreamed possible, and flashing signs of success may be important (hence, the sports car). At thirty-five, her values may shift to family and philanthropy. Her trip to Nepal may be replaced by a week in Disney World.

When a woman talks of some questionable item she is about to buy, embark on, or sink her savings into, I recommend a gut check regarding the values and goals she established to find out if anything has changed. If there has been a deviation from her values, she should say to herself, "Stop, breathe, and let's see how I feel. What is it about right now that makes me want to do this?"

The first consideration is whether her *situation* has genuinely changed. Is she exchanging one of her existing core values with a new one? Such changes are fairly unusual occurrences. More likely, emotions are obscuring the picture. If a potential financial move is surrounded by excitement, sadness, passion, or anxiety, chances are it is an *emotional* decision, not a conscious one.

High-running emotions can lead to powerful rationalization. But a woman won't know whether her new "great thing" will align with her core values until she first acknowledges which emotions are in play. This step is called a "purchase pause"—a breather that can prevent a great deal of loss and self-recrimination.

How to Take a Purchase Pause in Five Easy Steps

When you experience a deviation from your financial life plan, follow the steps below to readjust your lenses.

These steps are adapted from my larger-scope "The Four A's of Intentional Decision-Making" (see exhibit 3 in the resources at the back of this book).

1. **STOP, breathe, and feel:** Think about the proposed expenditure or action (buying the car, house, time-share, vacation home, business, investment, vacation, jewelry, etc.). What is the payoff experienced by doing this? How do you feel? Jot down your honest, private self-assessment so you can physically examine its reality. Examples: "I feel kind of desperate; if only I owned this, my life would be perfect." "I'm high with excitement—this stock option is a sure thing, and I'll make a fortune!" "I'm feeling cornered—if I don't agree to this vacation, my friends will lose interest in me."

2. **LOOK for the triggers:** Now consider *why* you are feeling the emotions you have recorded. *Is this an old behavior returning for the same old reasons?* If so, identify and write down those reasons. (Example: "I can slip into feelings of inadequacy when I am around wealthy, well-dressed women. It makes me want to run out and buy something expensive to make me feel worthy.") *If the emotions are new to you, try to identify what has triggered them.* Record your thoughts about returning or

new emotions. Next, record your ideas for keeping such emotions at bay. (Example: "My skills and strengths speak for themselves. I belong here, not because of what I wear but because of who I am and what I bring to the table.")

3. **IDENTIFY the real cost:** Beyond the payoff, there is a cost that is much greater. For example, the cost of buying a new item might be the additional credit card bill that comes in or the anxiety of knowing you will not be able to pay for an emergency expense. This cost is more precious, as it can have long-lasting effects on your self-worth. Keep the record of your revelations accessible to remind you of your particular vulnerability and how you overcame it.

4. **REVIEW previous decisions:** Once you have an understanding of the emotions and the payoff that influence your proposed behavior, you'll be equipped to review what you had previously decided was most important to you. Have the goals and values that were essential to your happiness and well-being really changed? Are you willing to enjoy the temporary payoff, even if the cost to your goals is more? Are you committed to modifying your behavior or giving up immediate temptations to attain your goals? If your values *have* changed, now is a great time to identify how they have changed and why.

5. **ALIGN with your goals and values:** If your values and goals have not changed, think about the action or purchase you are considering. How does that action align with it? If the action or purchase does not align,

pause to consider whether this is a good time to deviate from your values and goals.

6. **BE WILLING to forfeit.** If you choose to go ahead with your proposed action, accept that there may be a potential for gain (temporary payoff) but also a potential for loss (greater cost to self-worth and peace of mind). *If your values and goals have changed*, have a clear understanding of which previous goals you are replacing with new ones. If you accept your new goal, your next step is evaluating whether your new proposed action aligns with those changes. *If your values and goals have not changed*, reflect honestly about which goal you are willing to miss or value you are willing to compromise while taking whatever action you are considering.

WHAT IF I BACKSLIDE?

Habits, by their very definition, are hard to break. Backsliding after instituting any major behavioral change is not unusual. Early on, it is almost expected. Be kind to yourself. The good news is that, when slipping from the path of healthy physical or financial actions, there is almost always a chance to correct your behavior. Start by acknowledging the mistake. What happened? What could you have done differently? Then realign your actions with your values and goals and make a plan to move forward.

Anyone who has taken a self-defense class knows the best way to resolve a conflict is to avoid it in the first place. The finance equivalent of this is devising a *pre*plan for scenarios that would sabotage goals. For example, instead of succumbing to every cocktail outing because refusing is awkward, have a comfortable detour at the ready. Own the financial reality and possibly be an inspiration by saying you computed that cutting down on bar nights would net you over $3,000 a year, the price of the island vacation you've been dying to take. Would they like to join you for cocktails in Maui? (Or, nearer term, a theater night?)

An added bonus: your "plan ahead" strategy to prevent backsliding might offer a great example of how women can plan for long-term goals and support one another.

In Your Corner: Finding the Right Money Mentor

Finding an advocate to guide you through unexplored terrain in your relationship with money is crucial to solidifying your financial foundation. So, finding the right person is key. Think of this person as your "money mentor"—someone who not only has expertise in personal finance but may have even been in your position before. They're willing to tell you what you need to hear, when you need to hear it—even if you don't *want* to hear it. This person should really "get" you. Not only will they listen to and guide you; they'll hold you accountable when your actions aren't aligned with your goals.

GETTING SPECIFIC

Your best advocate will want to know all about *you*: how you think, behave, dream, and hope. How you use your money to help you achieve your needs in the present and the future. When you find the right advocate, use these tips as you work together.

1. **Work in tandem on the plan you have devised together.** Share what is working and not working regularly. When you clearly identify what is going well and what is not, you have an opportunity to leverage that into a more solid relationship. Create a cadence of communication that works for both of you. This will ensure you stay on track in a way that serves your goals and lifestyle.

2. **Don't be afraid to get real and confide in your advocate.** What might your modus operandi look like when you want to bail on your goals and action plans? Do you avoid the conversations that are bound to arise, make excuses, or shame yourself with guilt? Letting your advocate know how you typically respond will not only be helpful but give you both a chance to devise a plan for how to address it.

> **Confide in your advocate.**

YOUR ADVOCATE MUST EMBRACE WOMEN'S FINANCIAL AND LIFE ISSUES

Women tend to wear many hats, experience multiple income disruptions, and care for family members with little or no monetary remuneration. Because of these circumstances, women are especially prone to suffer financially when life tosses an *additional* situation into the picture—anticipated, unplanned, or even suddenly realized.

- **An expected event** can be joyful, like launching a new business or expecting a child, or painful, like a diagnosis of a terminal illness or dissolution of a marriage. Regardless, there is a chance to plan and prepare for the inevitable. There is an ability to process feelings in a different way when there is time to prepare. However, even expected events can negatively affect a woman's financial life plan because plans now have to alter course. When earning continuity is disrupted or changes to one's financial situation occur, insurance, retirement, and legacy planning can suffer.

- **An unplanned event** can be just as joyful or painful but often doesn't give adequate time to prepare or plan. These types of events can be financially disastrous as well, for all the ripple effects referenced above and more. What makes this even more complicated is that usually there is a whirlwind of emotions surrounding an unplanned event that have to be managed in connection with any financial decisions.

- **An aha moment** is a sudden realization—"Uh-oh, I need to be paying attention to my money and what's going on with it!" An aha moment can be triggered by events in a woman's own life or as she notes something going on in the world around her. She may sense her job is in jeopardy; a friend may go through a divorce and lose unprotected assets or become widowed and be left with reduced funds. In retirement, a woman may notice funds disappearing faster than anticipated for illness or family bailouts. Or she may look back and realize that a lifetime of scrimping has caused her to sacrifice things she might have embraced had she been better educated about managing her money.

Most female clients tell me that money management is "something I knew I should learn about one day." Or it's a subject so complicated by financial jargon and tax and investing issues that it never felt accessible to them. The truth is the right financial professional can help clients understand and digest information *as needed*. Together, advocate and client can devise a financial plan of attainable goals met through constructive, beneficial behaviors known in the vernacular as *good habits*. Ideally, good habits should be in place as early as possible, but it's never too late to start. The minute you do, you're course correcting right toward your goals.

YOUR ADVISOR AS HABIT BUILDER

Like everyone else, women need money in the bank. If Americans didn't grasp that reality before, they surely must now: after the early 2019 US government shutdown left thousands if not millions of American citizens financially damaged, a Federal Reserve survey revealed the unthinkable—almost *half* of Americans surveyed did not have enough money put aside to meet a $400 emergency.[4]

Yet anyone can save effectively by simply establishing good habits. Often, those habits entail little more than making a few behavioral changes—learning to take a financial time-out, for instance, before spending on a whim. Even building in a few fail-safe measures for yourself, such as putting money into an account that is not easily accessed, automatically creates the pause needed to reflect on whether an impulse or large purchase will delay you from getting to your goals.

Today, too many young people do not realize that their decisions to lease expensive cars, buy designer clothing, and rely on round-the-clock takeout are keeping them from building savings. This savings

---

4   Ylan Mui, "The Shocking Number of Americans Who Can't Cover a $400 Expense" *Washington Post*, April 29, 2019, https://www.washingtonpost.com/news/wonk/wp/2016/05/25/the-shocking-number-of-americans-who-cant-cover-a-400-expense/?noredirect=on&utm_term=.96c97450e45c.

could give them the liberty to handle emergencies, get out of a bad relationship, or change an unfulfilling job.

Therefore, *always pay yourself first*—the financial golden rule and an important habit to develop. Even if you take home $100 a week, you can give yourself $10 out of each paycheck toward financial security. By developing the pay-yourself-first savings habit, you'll never find yourself with only $400 to manage healthcare, home, job, auto, or family or relationship crises. You'll also avoid or ameliorate the risk of incurring credit card debt for life's unexpected, planned, and aha events—the kind of debt that can prevent you from achieving goals such as the following:

- Education to get a better job

- A down payment on a home

- World travel

- The ability to finance a new business

- The wherewithal to save for retirement

- (Add your own goals here)

This doesn't even take into account the price you pay with your personal health and well-being[5] as you suffer the stress that debt generates—and the "life cost" of that strain. Marriages break up over money worries, children struggle with anxiety when life at home does not feel secure, and opportunities for joy and memory building are sacrificed.

So what would you have to give up to save $5–$10 out of every $100? How would you be able to work with your new advocate to

---

5   Dyvonne Body and Financial Security Program, "The Burden of Debt on Mental and Physical Health," Aspen Institute, August 21, 2018, https://www.aspeninstitute.org/blog-posts/hidden-costs-of-consumer-debt/.

build the money habits that translate directly to meeting your life goals and living your values?

INVESTIGATE CREDENTIALS

As in every marketplace, the caution is always "buyer beware." In healthcare, for instance, you'd certainly want the best-credentialed physician with the utmost experience. Even home construction and car repair require thorough vetting: your home is your most major investment, and you rely on your auto to safely transport family and friends.

Yet when it comes to finances, people will turn over the care and feeding of their life savings, investments, and retirement funds to an individual recommended by a friend of a friend or to someone who offered a free dinner for the opportunity to deliver a presentation. Nothing is inherently wrong with either of these scenarios as long as you thoroughly check credentials, experience, reviews, professional background, and industry-required disclosures (via industry and professional organizations) before you sign on any dotted line. With a little insider information in your pocket, you'll know precisely what to look for. Check out the following pointers to manage your due diligence like a pro.

Education, Certifications, Designations, and Licenses

Although there are different *required* standards for financial advisors depending on the type of advice you get, you will want to look for key indicators, such as certifications and designations, that let you know you are dealing with a financial professional.

To view education and certifications, go to the advisor's business website, LinkedIn, or Facebook page and to industry websites such as finra.org (Financial Industry Regulatory Authority).[6] You can find out most of what you need to know about your potential advisor via FINRA's BrokerCheck website at https://brokercheck.finra.org/.

Many financial professionals receive their degrees from universities or colleges, but not all do. Often, advisors will list their majors or areas of study to demonstrate their focus on finance. As for certifications and designations, advisors can be certified in specific areas (see the box below to crack the code of meaningful designations). Remember, designations also indicate how much education your financial planning professional *continues* to pursue!

Consider comprehensive planning, for instance: an advisor certified in that wide-reaching focus will be working to make sure you are at the very least covered by all needed types of insurance; have testamentary, trust, and health instruments in place; and have secured diversified retirement and growth investments.

Your investment advisor must be licensed by your state to sell or recommend products. The licenses should reflect that your portfolio manager has passed appropriate exams (I look for series 6, 7, 63, 65, and 66). If not licensed, they must refer you to another professional.

Financial advisors are not ordinarily attorneys, so if needed, many will be able to either refer you to a qualified legal professional or direct you to sources for locating one. Your goal: to build your best possible financial dream team.

Finally, be wary of online money gurus who have no credentials but insist they are qualified to tell you what to do with your money! They may know next to nothing about your personal situation— and may be giving general advice that won't work for you. Because noncredentialed advisors answer to no regulating authority, they are

---

6   Other helpful financial industry websites include www.nasaa.org (North American Securities Administrators Association and www.nfa.futures.org (National Futures Association).

53

under no obligation whatsoever to be held responsible for the advice they give you. Beware!

Which Financial Advocate Is Right for You?

CFP—Certified Financial Planner. Most widely recognized credential in financial planning. The rigorous certification requirements ensure you are in the best financial planning hands.

ChFC—Chartered Financial Consultant. This designation contains much of the same education as the CFP but is offered through the American College of Financial Services. Those who complete the CLU and ChFC exams can also qualify to sit for the CFP exam.

CFA—Chartered Financial Analyst. In terms of investment management, stringent academic requirements for those who have a need for advanced investment analysis and real-world portfolio management skills.

CPFA—Certified Plan Fiduciary Advisor. A CPFA will not only work with you on your retirement plan but, as a fiduciary,[7] has officially pledged to protect your financial interests and rights.

CIC—Chartered Investment Counselor. An advisor with

---

7   According to BusinessDictionary.com, "The law demands a fiduciary to exercise highest degree of care and utmost good faith in maintenance and preservation of the principal's assets and rights, and imposes compensatory as well as punitive damages on the erring fiduciary."

this designation is schooled and experienced in portfolio management—important for those who will diversify their assets. A financial planner need not also be a CIC but can refer you to a top-level, local professional and work in tandem with him or her.

Specialized Planning

CDFA—Certified Divorce Financial Analyst. A very helpful professional for those facing separation and divorce. A CDFA will employ deep knowledge of tax law and asset distribution to inform clients about divorce settlement options. Again, your certified financial planner can help you add this valuable individual to your planning team.

RICP—Retirement Income Certified Professional. Women nearing or already in retirement often wonder if they will be OK throughout their later years. For those individuals especially, the RICP designation is a valuable addition to their financial planner's roster of certifications. This certification ensures realistic management and spend-down of the assets that have been accumulated for retirement.

CRPC—Chartered Retirement Planning Counselor. For clients of *any* age, an advisor with the CRPC certification will focus on needs both before *and* after retirement. Those professionals with CRPC designations will help to define and design a successful retirement blueprint.

CRPS—Chartered Retirement Plans Specialist. You may never need an advisor with this certification, yet if you own a business with employees, you could; this financial specialist creates and maintains retirement plans for businesses.

CLU—Chartered Life Underwriter. Because the financial benefits of life insurance products may be essential to your financial blueprint for the future, an individual holding this designation could be a valuable addition to your financial team.

BFA—Behavioral Financial Advisor. This designation could bring a critical improvement to both your financial present *and* future. Simply put, an advisor with a BFA certification helps clients manage their emotions and improve their investment and money-management decision-making behavior.

ChSNC—Chartered Special Needs Consultant. This designation brings an expertise to those dealing with loved ones who have special needs. This includes specialization in Medicaid, Medicare, Social Security, and trust planning.

Should You Ask a Friend?

While we all like getting recommendations from friends, be careful here. Just because your friend is happy with her financial professional doesn't mean they will be appropriate for *you*. Even your best friends and family may have different goals and expectations than you do. So when querying others for personal recommendations, ask these six important questions:

- What do you know about your financial professional's credentials and certifications?

- How well do you think your financial professional understands your personal situation, values, and behavior?

- How has your financial professional helped you prepare for emergencies and contingencies?

- What personal characteristics does your financial professional have that appeal to you most?

- How frequently does your financial professional reach out to you?

- How responsive is your financial professional to *your* outreach?

Questions to Ask Yourself before You Choose an Advocate

Most of us think that the questions we ask a professional are the most important, but, in actuality, the questions we ask ourselves *first* lay the groundwork for the interview to come. Check out these basic self-assessment considerations, then add your own.

- **Where am I NOW in my life and my finances?** Will I be able to effectively and truthfully describe what that looks like? Imagining that my life has its own GPS system and I need to use it to get where I want to go financially, will I be able to clearly input my *current* location? (Hint: I won't be able to get anywhere else if I don't know my starting point.)

- **What is my style of working with advising professionals?** Am I a self-starter, preferring an educational session or two before I take it from there? Do I look for more consistent monitoring via an accountability partner? Would I appreciate a schedule of ongoing check-ins and some hand-holding along the way? Or am I typically a more skeptical personality seeking to challenge as needed?

- **How often would I meet or communicate with an advocate** to help establish a solid financial strategy and adopt better financial habits? What would be my preferred mode of communication?

- **How will I probably behave when I fall off my financial plan wagon?** Will I enable or hinder my financial advocate to help me to get back on track? Am I able to look at my potentially undesirable behavior, own it, and ask for help when I need it most?

Questions to Ask a Potential Financial Advocate

Most people have no problem asking financial professionals how they get paid. The key is to find someone who cares about you and has a high level of integrity as well as moral and behavioral competency. Will they do the right thing for *you*? Take your time when you interview. Don't be afraid to ask the following:

- **How long have you been in this business?** If they are new, do they have a team that can help with oversight for your situation? If they have been in the business for a while, are they up on all current planning techniques and products?

- **What do most of your clients say about working with you?** May I speak with a few of your clients?

- **What values are most important to you?** You want to find someone who will appreciate your values and respect them. Knowing theirs gives you an indication as to whether they have thought about their own and if they resonate with you.

- **Can you share with me a time when a client asked you to take a particular action** and you knew it was not in your client's best interest? How did you handle this?

- **How do you handle working with difficult clients?** Ask for a couple of examples.

- **Please tell me about a time when you made a mistake** and how you resolved that situation.

- **How often would you expect to meet or communicate with me** to help me establish a solid financial strategy and adopt better financial habits? (Once a month or more to establish goals and an action plan? Once a year?) Would you work within my preferred mode of communication?

- **What types of fee structures do you use and why?** (Fee structures can vary widely from annual portfolio percentages to flat fees or fee payment plans.) How will you charge me for your services? Is there any room for negotiation?

Above all, do not be intimidated by "financial speak"! If you do not understand something, don't be afraid to stop and ask for clarification. And feel free to call out intimidating behavior by interjecting, "I'm sorry, but what you're saying doesn't mean anything to me. Can you put this in a context that would mean something to my situation?" Don't be afraid to stand up for yourself! This is *your* life, *your* money, and *your* future. You have the right to ask any question for which you need an answer, and you have the right to request clarity. If a prospective advocate is not able to leave the industry jargon, demographics, and financial terminology at the door, he or she is probably not the professional for you.

Women are naturally relationship oriented, so you'll want a

financial advocate who probes deeply, asking plenty of questions about *you*. You want someone who conveys, "I'm in this with you, and we're going to figure this out together. It's not about me telling you what to do. It's about working as a team. We'll go as slowly as we need to for you to feel good about what we're doing."

Keep in mind that although many financial professionals like to educate clients about virtually every product imaginable, you don't need to become an expert on all products. You just need to know how that product will work for you and why it's a good choice for your situation.

Having said all that, when women learn bit by bit about specific investment categories, they tend to become quite interested and ask extremely intelligent questions. In fact, women often ask more questions than men! These days, women want to make sure they are not investing in products that contradict their belief systems (products offered by companies supporting child labor, rainforest destruction, or the proliferation of arms, for instance). Some female clients like to do their own research on companies or even tour facilities.

Not surprisingly, because women choose their positions carefully—and then stay with them—they often become better at investing than men. As for working with an advocate, because men are not as relationship focused as women, they're more likely to sprint through consultation sessions—and through investment positions too. Taking the time to go as slow as you need can allow you to feel more confident in your decisions.

WHAT ABOUT SALLY?

Our composite Sally met weekly with the professional she had chosen to get up and running; she then set up a check-in schedule so her advocate could keep on top of things too. Though Sally did hit a snag here and there, she didn't need to hide her slipups because she had adequately prepared for them and knew they were human.

In the end, she hit her goals—and then some. She became so independent she traveled all over the world, contributed to her church, and even set up a community scholarship fund that bears her name. She has prized the financial security she created and maintained to enable her visions. Today, Sally looks ahead to retirement without fear and is reviewing plenty of exciting options. All of this came about because she practiced three essential Ps: she got in touch with her priorities, imagined her possibilities, and got present in her life.

Under the Influence: Money Beliefs and Habits You Don't Even Realize You Picked Up in Childhood

Not uncommonly, siblings exposed to identical childhood influences often use them in different ways to create the foundations of their unique lives and form their relationships with money. One child may incorporate early influences of frugality (say, hand-me-down clothes and childhood lessons about saving money) to build a life of acquiring, protecting, and optimizing money and assets. The other may find happiness, serenity, and security in the straightforward, uncomplicated life of economy inherited from parents. Anyone who has ever worked with an empathy map (see below) can quickly see how what our parents told us may have influenced us in very different ways.

Parents may say identical things to each child, yet each child may think, feel, and act quite differently.

Empathy Map

The four quadrants of an empathy map

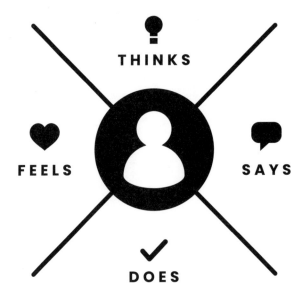

THINKS

FEELS

SAYS

DOES

OUR PARENTS, OURSELVES

The important thing is to know *why* we have the money relationships that we have. Often, it is interesting to look not just at how various siblings in the same family respond to their parents' attitudes toward money but at how whole generations react to the way their parents reared them. Not surprisingly, children throughout history have balked at their upbringing and responded by heading (at least initially) in the opposite direction. The children of sacrificing Depression-era parents were upwardly mobile and consumer driven, spending their post-WWII dollars on homes, cars, the latest conveniences, vacations, country clubs, and whatever else their budding prosperity could provide. Their children, the boomers, openly rebelled against their parents' materialism by launching a hippie generation that decried material possessions. Then, as boomers became breadwinners and parents, they paradoxically became even more money and status driven than the generation before them. Recently, many millennials have reacted to their overproviding helicopter parents by seeking an experiential, nomadic existence. It is one not dependent on home and car ownership, traditional mores, or even time-honored institutions or societal norms. Yet as they, too, become parents, some of the millennial money and life attitudes are now shifting, and the conversations about these changes play out in the press and on the internet daily.

> Recently, many millennials have reacted to their overproviding helicopter parents by seeking an experiential, nomadic existence.

My brother and I, for instance, think often about the influences of our upbringing on our attitudes and behaviors around money. We look at our reactions, checking in with them and tweaking them along the way. Though years ago in our community, people did not discuss money, in our family, we *did* and do still. My brother and I were fortunate: we talk about what money means to us, what our dreams and aspirations look like, and how money can make those dreams come to life. Years ago, each of us in our own way started that conversation with ourselves, and it has never ended. In fact, our most important step was to *start* the conversation, which can never come too late.

What Shaped Your Ideas about Money and You?

For starters, ask yourself the following questions. Then share the resulting responses with your advocate, or ponder them to gain fresh insight about what may be behind your current money maxim.

1. **Did your parents talk to you about money, or was there family silence on the subject?** If your parents talked about money, what did they say? (Examples: "Money is to be saved, not spent." "Money is to be enjoyed, not hoarded." "People who spend their money will end up in the poorhouse." "You only live once; treat yourself!") Were you allowed or encouraged to ask questions about money?

2. **Did you hear your parents speak with each other about money?** If so, what did they express to each other? Did your mother and father have different attitudes about money? How did they refer to each other's spending or money management efforts?

3. **What did you like about your parents' attitude toward money?** What did you dislike?

4. **What was the community attitude toward money where you grew up?**

5. **Did your family fit in with community money standards?** If not, how did the community let your family know that you did not fit in? Did that make an impression on your beliefs about money? If so, how?

6. **If you answered no to question 5, how did that make you feel?** Describe your feelings as completely as you can.

7. **When was the first time you believed that money could buy (or help you to gain) things such as acceptance, friendship, and popularity?** When you were young, what did money mean to you (other than being a direct means of exchange for goods and services)?

8. **When you thought about being a grown-up, how did you envision the perfect grown-up life?** Home, cars, career? Nomadic and experiential? Consumer driven? Consumer averse?

9. **Can you see a connection between your upbringing and your current attitude about money?**

10. **Is your reaction to your parents' money attitudes the same** as your own *authentic* feelings about your money and your life goals? If not, how do the feelings differ?

11. **Did your parents ever come to regret their attitudes about money?** (Examples: "I wish we had saved more." "I wish we had enjoyed ourselves more.")

12. **Do you ever have conversations about the above issues?** If so, with whom do you discuss your money attitudes or feelings about money management?

LET'S TALK ABOUT MONEY AND POWER

Not long ago I heard the story of a businesswoman who had been rear-ended in her brand-new little Lexus by a young receptionist driving a big new Mercedes. It turned out that the young woman at fault had found a way to splurge on her pricey vehicle but had inadequately insured it to save money.

When I heard this account, I had to wonder why anyone would funnel her annual income into such a lavish car and then underinsure it, *leaving herself open to litigation that could damage her life*. No, the Lexus owner didn't sue, but her insurance company had to pursue the other driver's carrier for ample compensation. That altered the young woman's insurance rates, which squeezed her monthly expenses, which reduced her discretionary spending, which affected her ability to go out to dinner, travel, shop, and—well, you get the picture.

All told, the decision to opt for a flashy car and then sacrifice the security of adequate accident insurance was certainly costlier than anticipated.

Or had she not considered the possible repercussions, making her decisions only with her emotions? Had the young receptionist purchased her Mercedes the way another young woman might have splurged on $800 Louboutins? Or maybe she was sucked in by the purchasing pressure of the internet, where every female can appear successful, smart, and stylish instantly. With the ease of buying anything these days, it is not uncommon for many to get carried away with purchasing so they can appear to be living their best life all while sacrificing real enjoyment. When myWorth asked site users to reveal the one thing they spent the least amount of money for, but received the most value from, they chose time with family and friends. Given that, perhaps it is time we reevaluate our priorities and change how we are spending our money.

After hearing about the domino effect this accident had on the unwitting receptionist's life, my reaction was: Did the young woman understand that when she shelled out $60,000 for her impressive new car and then underinsured it, *she also relinquished her power to control life's inevitable crises—like an auto accident?*

Maybe the real question is: What's the true relationship between your money and your power? When you think of the relationship between money and power, what comes to mind? Great wealth and societal influence? Corporate and political power? Or the power to forge your own path?

It may surprise you, but the real power of money has less to do with wielding power and amassing wealth than it has to do with appreciating money as *a tool primed with the power to propel you toward your life's authentic goals.*

Certainly those goals could align with core values such as wealth and/or power, but as we have found at myWorth, most women's life goals are more likely to align with security, freedom, independence, and accomplishment.

Studies of lottery winners show that the acquisition of wealth in itself does not make for happiness; in fact, the reverse tends to be true.[8] People need an ability to *understand* money and its relationship to human goals and aspirations to positively influence their lives. One

> **People need an ability to *understand* money and its relationship to human goals and aspirations to positively influence their lives.**

---

8   Melissa Chan, "Powerball: How Winning the Lottery Makes You Miserable," *Time*, January 12, 2016, http://time.com/4176128/powerball-jackpot-lottery-winners/.

lottery winner backed this up when he said, "Hire a good financial planner and a good accountant after paying off all debts. People, they just don't think. You have to secure your future."[9]

To assist winners, many state lotteries offer payouts in the form of annuities that will secure winners' futures and prevent them from running through their fortunes.[10] The National Football League, too, requires *certified* financial planning to accompany the mammoth compensation packages its teams award young recruits. This is an effort to prevent the many life disasters the league has already witnessed when the young players fall into the hands of unscrupulous "advisors."[11] The fact is, those who have never been exposed to affluence—whether male or female—can drown in a sudden tsunami of wealth.

Were I advising lottery winners, I would suggest they allocate a modest percentage of funds for "going a little crazy" and enjoying the excitement of their win. (Think about it: What would be your "go-crazy" purchase?) Then I would help them get down to the business of securing their future by strategizing a plan to achieve their unique goals. We would also revisit the initial thrilling expenditures a few months later to see if those purchases were as life changing as anticipated or just a novelty to own. You'd be amazed how many people actually believe that purchasing a big house or acquiring an expensive sports car will turn them into more self-assured individuals. They're always surprised to discover that they're still the same people—with less money in the bank.

---

9   Chan, writing about Richard Lustig, one of the rare individuals financially healthy and happy after his lottery windfall.

10   Stan Garrison Haithcock, "Why Lottery Winners Should Choose the Annuity, Not the Lump Sum," Balance, July 30, 2019, https://www.thebalance.com/annuity-not-lump-sum-145904.

11   Jeff Benjamin, "NFL Wants Advisers to Have CFP or CFA Designation to Work with Players," *InvestmentNews*, June 18, 2018, https://www.investmentnews.com/article/20180618/FREE/180619924/nfl-wants-advisors-to-have-cfp-or-cfa-designation-to-work-with.

Has Your Go-Crazy Purchase Changed Your Life for the Better? Five Questions

You already know how to take a pause *before* you make an impulsive purchase to check in with your motives, emotions, and the goals that you had previously examined and determined. But how do you feel *after* shelling out for a go-crazy purchase or something you were certain would bring you happiness, confidence, admirers, or the life of your dreams? To gauge the true value of a splurge, ask yourself these five questions after the deed has been done:

1. How did I feel when I first made my purchase or expenditure? (Examples: excited, high, floating, guilty, worried, panicky, numb)

2. How did I feel about the purchase or expenditure a few weeks later? (Examples: just as excited, thrilled with the purchase, proud of the purchase, depressed, remorseful, panicky, numb)

3. Did my purchase or expenditure change my life for the better? For the worse? Not at all?

4. What are my thoughts today regarding the worth of this expenditure versus continuing toward my goals?

5. How is this purchase related to my childhood attitudes toward money?

Windfalls aside, within the general population, males are still more likely to take a more active role in their financial lives than women (although that is changing).[12] That may be because boys are taught about money earlier than girls are. Even anecdotally, women know that male children receive signals early on prompting them to understand and harness the power of their money, to help them achieve success and impress and attract others, especially mates.

It's no surprise then that, as males mature, many tune in to information that will help them put their funds to work for them, increase their net worth, and give them the freedom to do as they wish. Certainly, their interest in the power of money can sometimes lead to *poor* money management—gambling, for instance. Still, most males are motivated to manage their money better than they innately do. If they can't figure it out themselves, they'll enlist the aid of others, hire professionals, or learn about online trading in their spare time. *Managing their money is important to men.*

In fact, women often wonder how it is that men they know are able to retire *early*, while they worry they won't have adequate funds even at full retirement age. I recently heard the story of a warm and happy family wherein the father was able to retire at fifty. The woman who told me this story remarked that the family lives in a modest home with Toyotas in the driveway. She assumed these were simple people with only basic needs and that the father must have been lucky enough to have a pension or a good government job. Was she surprised to find out that he had been a hedge fund manager! Just like some of the individuals chronicled in *The Millionaire Next Door*,[13] he had decided that his life's goal was to enjoy his family while he was young. That goal was much more important to the

---

12   Marguerita Cheng, "Women Need to Take a More Active Role in Their Financial Lives," CNBC, April 30, 2018, https://www.cnbc.com/2018/04/30/women-need-to-take-an-active-role-in-their-financial-lives.html.

13   Thomas J. Stanley and William D. Danko, *The Millionaire Next Door: The Surprising Secrets of America's Wealthy* (Lanham, MD: Taylor Trade Publishing, 2016).

entire family than living large.

Today, women are also substantial contributors to the family income through successful careers of their own. They may even hold the higher-paying job. Yet they are still largely responsible for raising the couple's children, maintaining the family home, and transacting the family's needed expenditures. Women often say they simply don't have the time to pursue financial knowledge and instead rely on their *partner's* acquired knowledge of money management (whether it turns out to be reliable knowledge or not). Many even intend to learn more about finance one day and feel guilty that they've not yet pursued such education.

The question is, Why aren't women more motivated to seize the power of managing their own money?

As women, we acquire and exercise confidence and experience in the home, workplace, political arena, and in relationships. We could certainly gain the experience and confidence needed to manage our own financial security and freedom and achieve our personal goals and aspirations. So, why are we willing to surrender our power to intelligently manage our own finances? While we can accept that much of what we learned about money we learned in childhood, our conversations about our money must progress to this affirmation: today, as adult women, understanding and harnessing the power of our money will give us more effective control of our lives.

JOY THROUGH TIDYING UP: BETTER LATE THAN NEVER

Then there is something we may *not* have learned in childhood: how reducing the clutter of things that don't bring us joy can also keep us financially healthy. Marie Kondo, author of *The Life-Changing Magic of Tidying Up*, maintains that we must find joy in what we accumulate. I agree with her and believe that clutter turns into noise that disrupts the peace of our lives and prevents us from seeing our life paths.

> **Have your finances become a "junk drawer" that makes it impossible for you to see where your dollars are going?**

It's the same with money and finances. Have your finances become a "junk drawer" that makes it impossible for you to see where your dollars are going? Or are your finances tidily allocated into accessible slots for protection, savings, growth, and debt—a drawer you can access and work with anytime you choose? Are you deriving *joy* from each of your five Spotify accounts or the numerous streaming services you have (or the ten pairs of black pants you have in your closet)?

We absorb more in childhood than our parents' values about life and money; we pick up good habits and bad. Those habits can pervade all the areas of our lives as we mature, while we don't think to stop and ask ourselves: Is what I am doing bringing me joy? Learning good financial habits and tidying them up occasionally is not just something you *should* do; strong, tidy habits will build your road to security, fulfillment, and joy.

The bottom line is *women need to learn about their money and their worth just as men do*. Though it is never too late to learn, new generations of women are entitled to learn early and learn well, building both solid and tidy financial habits that will help them realize their power to direct their life goals.

All Grown Up: What an Adult Relationship to Money Should Look Like

Letting go of some of the things you learned about money in childhood is a *good* thing. That's because adults can make of their lives what they wish, not what anyone else—their parents, community, or society—decides for them. Today, all that any adult woman needs to help her financially meet her life vision is a system tailored for *her*.

ADULTS SEEK QUALIFIED ASSISTANCE

As people mature, most come to understand that though life can seem overwhelming at times, there's a system for just about every-thing—a system that helps busy adults "chunk down" tasks into digestible steps. The same is true of money management and the many things related to it. Many adults come to realize that they can rely on the assistance of professionals of all kinds to help them navigate the more complex passages of their lives: healthcare and mental health experts, legal advisors, accounting professionals, marriage and family counselors, auto service pros, nutritional advisors, weight trainers, beauty practitioners, and more. Professionals also exist who are well equipped to assist adults with the management of money and finances and all the life issues that intersect with them (see "In Your Corner: Finding the Right Money Mentor").

Yet it's necessary to add here that in the financial planning world, we now have a greater understanding of the importance of emotionally connecting with clients and the stresses and conflicts they face. This is especially true vis-à-vis the needs of female clients, who are often put off by the "don't worry; I've got this" attitude that men more often appreciate.

> **Women must find financial advocates who are not only sympathetic to their issues but, ideally, empathetic as well.**

Women, however, tend to look for professionals who understand their concerns and can identify with a woman's unique position in the world. Women must find financial advocates who are not only sympathetic to their issues but, ideally, empathetic as well. In her best seller *Dare to Lead*, University of Houston research professor Brené Brown points out that sympathy is feeling *for* someone's circumstance, while empathy is feeling that circumstance *with* them.

Finding solid and expert financial advice that is also empathetic is goal one. A responsible adult won't wait for a crisis to seek out professional help from an advocate who says—and means—"I'm right there with you on your journey to find the power of your money."

THE MEANING OF RESPONSE-ABILITY

How important is it for women to own response-ability: the *ability* to be financially responsible for their own lives? Simply put, it's essential.

Melissa always believed herself blessed to have married a doctor. Her life was one she had imagined: beautiful children, lovely home, no shortage of luxuries. She never had to worry about money, and she was delighted her husband managed everything so she didn't have to deal with "all those details." She trusted him completely, which left her free to handle children, home, and life for everyone else.

Then came the divorce. Because she never reviewed the couple's financial papers (or even asked to see them), what Melissa had not known was that her husband had placed all their assets in *her* name to protect his medical practice. She was forced to declare bankruptcy as all accumulated debt (of which there was plenty, but how could she know?) attached to her, not him. His practice (and livelihood) remained untouched while she and the children became victims of financial devastation. "I trusted him! I didn't know any better!" Melissa admitted.

Sadly, I hear the same type of story all the time from women who literally banked their lives on their long marriages and devoted spouses. There was the young wife and mother whose stock-trader husband was secretly funding his trading account with credit card loans he took out under *her* name. (Divorce, bankruptcy, and foreclosure followed while he departed for greener pastures). And then there was the couple who had been married for almost fifty years when he died suddenly of heart failure—and she discovered they had been living on client money her estate-attorney husband had quietly "borrowed" from their estates, intending to pay it back. Had she simply reviewed a joint tax return, she might have noticed a disparity in earned income and their spending habits. But since she didn't, at seventy-five she was left to face the consequences.

Were these women unsophisticated or uneducated? No; all three women were accomplished, capable individuals who, in managing home and hearth, had unwittingly surrendered their *ability to be responsible* for a huge portion of their lives: their finances. Exercising or surrendering that responsibility would affect almost every corner of their lives. Furthermore, what happened to these women was not so much about marrying the right or wrong people. It was about relinquishing their responsibility to take care of *themselves* while they were acting as caretakers for others.

> When a woman takes responsibility for her own finances (and thus her own life), she is acknowledging that her life is her own to direct as she sees fit.

When a woman takes responsibility for her own finances (and thus her own life), she is acknowledging that her life is her own to direct as she sees fit. She is acknowledging that she is an adult who does not need to cede her innate rights and power to others. *Every* woman of sound mind needs to know what is going on with her own assets! Being an adult means that you need to know about adult things, including how to manage your money.

Men need to be responsible for themselves too—they need to know how to cook for themselves and others, shop for food, do laundry, tidy up a home, and more. Men and women alike need to know how to manage *both* sides of life, to affirm to themselves that they are responsible adults who can take care of themselves. Everyone needs to understand the importance of *self*-care.

In fact, many men today want to ensure that the women in their lives (daughters and mothers) know how to manage their finances. They ask, "How can my daughter learn about money as she moves into the world? How can I make sure no one will take advantage of her and that she will not marry to have someone else manage her life?" In the same vein, they want to know, "How can my mother be better educated about money in case she is alone?"

These concerns are genuine but not entirely altruistic—after all, those in the sandwich generation can visualize the impact on their own lives as both daughters *and* mothers require financial assistance at the same time! Remember, the ripple effect of financial calamity often expands to others in a family.

KNOW YOUR VALUE OR PAY LATER

In the first two conversations of this book, we discussed at length a woman's challenges in assessing her value, since her value is not always easy to evaluate. Yet why is the actual *computation* of a woman's value so important? For these two reasons:

What Are You Worth to Your Family?

First, a woman needs to understand the *way* her worth will be computed so that she is not blindsided at retirement or at the onset of a long-term illness, for instance. Her family, too, may need recompense for her value (what she contributes to the daily operation of the family) should she suddenly be disabled or deceased.

If she were seriously injured, who would take care of her? Or the children? How would the family pay for her day-to-day care? How would the family and household function without her, so that her husband or partner could continue to work and support the family?

How would she be able to continue her level of independence if remaining single by choice?

If marital dissolution is at hand, what would her value amount to *in her particular state* as a settlement is negotiated during a divorce? What if she had worked to support the family for years while her husband attended professional school? What if her efforts to find a home, furnish it, maintain it, and entertain her husband's clients were instrumental in his success? And what of her value in being the primary caretaker of the couple's children—say, if she had given up her own career and interrupted her earning years to raise a family?

Just as importantly, what happens to a woman's retirement income if she has interrupted or sacrificed her own earning potential for reasons beneficial to the family?

All these questions make it clear that a woman's value may be more difficult to compute than a man's; nevertheless, her worth should be represented by a monetary value not only so that recompense can be attained when most needed, but so that—along with her financial advocate—she can plot out her financial strategy, early on, to *protect* her life's value!

What Are You Worth to Your Community and to Society?

The second reason a woman's value needs to be assessed is one often overlooked: What is her value to her community and society as a whole? This is important because countless studies reveal that in our society, *women are more likely to suffer financial hardship* as a result of marital or partnership dissolution, medical debt, or overspending. Yet when a woman understands her true value to society, she is more likely to carefully assess her worth and protect it.

After all, if she is working, she is contributing tax dollars to her city, state, and federal government. She is supporting the financial health of her community and national economy, purchasing groceries, gas, going out to eat, and more. Her money continually flows through the economy at large, and her contribution is not minor.[14] Yet, if she suffers financial hardship, that personal hardship also affects society as a whole—including these two just for starters:

- **Charitable donations suffer too.** Sixty-four percent of donations are made by women, according to Nonprofit Source.[15] As women face financial hardship, philanthropy across the board feels their pain.

- **Millennial women in the United States are putting off or not having children.**[16] These young women are the first generation to grapple with financial and housing hardships their mothers did not face. If they believe they cannot afford to have children, how will that financially motivated decision affect their lives? And what will be the ripple effects on countless markets serving 15 percent fewer US consumers (unborn children) in the coming years?

---

14 According to the *Harvard Business Review*, women influence almost 85 percent of all consumer spending in the United States, now over $8 trillion annually (larger than the economies of China and India combined!). At *HBR*'s last accounting, women make the decision in the purchases of 94 percent of home furnishings, 92 percent of vacations, 91 percent of homes, 60 percent of automobiles, and 51 percent of consumer electronics.

15 "The Ultimate List of Charitable Giving Statistics for 2018," Nonprofits Source, accessed November 12, 2019, https://nonprofitssource.com/online-giving-statistics/.

16 Bee Gray, "Financial Hardship Plays a Major Role in Why Millennial Women Are Putting Off Pregnancy," *BUST*, https://bust.com/living/14110-financial-hardship-plays-a-major-role-in-why-millennial-women-are-putting-off-pregnancy.html.

APPROPRIATELY EVALUATING YOUR WORTH MATTERS TOO

It is a woman's own responsibility to make sure that she does not underestimate her worth to family and community and thus impair her ability to *personally* thrive and succeed in the present and beyond.

As a woman, appropriately evaluating your worth means that you assess not only your current earning power but your *future* potential for earning as well. This is how a life insurance agent would compute your worth over your lifetime. It is not needs-based planning (multiplying what you need right now over a set period of years) but more like space planning, wherein a business owner chooses space not for the first year of operation but for function down the line as the business grows.

For a woman, needs-based planning would be planning for the lowest denominator—where she is right now. Yet looking ahead to future aspirations and circumstances is *not* pie-in-the-sky thinking! A woman must also plan for her needs and dreams to come, or those things may never become realities, especially as the world around her changes in unforeseen ways.

Even a twenty-five-year-old currently making only $25,000 a year would have a lifetime earning value of a million dollars projected over forty years. But $25,000 is only a *starting* income. With potential wage increases and opportunities for career growth, that woman's earning *potential* will likely grow. When thinking about your worth, consider your most valuable asset is your ability to earn an income. Protecting that should be a high priority.

Procrastination (I'll think about financial planning when I get married … when I have children … when the kids are in school … as soon as this divorce is final) is the enemy, gobbling up not just interest and investment growth but dreams. Are women simply not concerned about their financial futures?

They are concerned. When myWorth anecdotally surveyed two hundred women visiting the website in 2018–2019 to find out what kept them up at night, the overwhelming response was some form of "I want to know that I will be OK." They worried about being dependent upon others, becoming a burden, or even ending up as a bag lady. In fact, I don't recall a response that varied from the desire to be protected from financial adversity.

GIVING BACK FOR GROWN-UPS AND THEIR FAMILIES

Many adults do not feel their lives are balanced without some form of giving back to those outside of family, be it community or society at large. If this is important to you, work with your financial advocate to devise a plan for donating monetarily. Then consider alternative ways to make a difference for others. You can, for example, gradually work up to 10 percent church tithing if that level of contributing is important to you. But you can also find *non*monetary ways to give back to your church or community, by volunteering or launching much-needed community programs. And giving back isn't only for grown-ups; parents and their children alike can review the family's annual gift-giving expenditures and repurpose hundreds or thousands of dollars spent on gifts to donate to favorite charities instead. Teaching your children "grown-up" giving also helps to create more balanced generations of future adults.

WORKING FOR YOURSELF

For many, the ultimate symbol of arriving at financial adulthood is the decision to launch one's own business or become self-employed, and more women now choose to work for themselves than ever before.[17] Working for yourself can be quite different than working for someone else. Just make sure to build a team of advisors you can trust. And don't overlook freelancing, partnering, e-commerce, blogging and podcasting, and helpful platforms like KickStart that will help you test your products and services before you launch.

Build a team of advisors you can trust.

QUICK START TO A RESPONSE-ABLE FINANCIAL FOUNDATION

In the following chapter, we'll talk about some of the most important actions and documents related to the critical areas of your personal finances. As we move through the specific items in that chapter, you'll be able to identify (1) many of the documents you already have in place, plus (2) the documents that are missing, which you will need to add.

To quick start your financial document organization and review, complete the following steps:

---

17   Team Everlance, "2018 Self-Employment Statistics in the US," *Everlance* (blog), June 7, 2018, https://www.everlance.com/blog/self-employment-statistics/. In 2015, 7.4 percent of US men were among the ranks of the unincorporated self-employed, compared with 5.2 percent of women. The incorporated self-employment rate for US men was 4.9 percent, compared with 2.3 percent for women. Though more recent statistics are wanting, experts say the gaps between men and women are narrowing.

First, simply gather your existing financial documents. (If possible, invite your financial advocate to review the documents as you proceed. He or she can help you quickly organize your strategic financial documents. But don't wait—if you don't have an advocate, you can still get started on your own.)

Second, on a roomy table or surface, place marked sticky notes of the five categories for organization listed below.

Third, review and categorize your documents. (You can download coverage summaries from your online user portals if you do not have hard copies.)

Categories for organization include the following:

1. **Keep:** Is this strategy working well for me and fine just the way it is?

2. **Eliminate:** Are certain products I own (financial, insurance, etc.) no longer of use to me and my plans? Should I reallocate the money I am spending on these products to buy what I am missing?

3. **Modify or Replace:** Would this strategy work better for me with updating, revision, or improvement? Are there improved products or options now available? (A good financial advocate will keep up on the latest options to maximize protection or financial growth opportunities.)

4. **Revisit:** If this strategy is fine for now, does it need to be tagged for revisiting in six months, a year, or two years?

5. **What's Missing?** Looking at my financial products, is there an important component missing? Am I appropriately insured to protect not just my health and home but my *ability to earn an income*? Are my retirement accounts diversified to ensure my retirement income is optimized,

not jeopardized? (Here's where a financial advocate can be helpful—this is the assessment most difficult for nonprofessionals and often the most eye opening as well.)

Once you've organized your financial documents to reveal the true status of your financial response-ability, you're ready to discuss the five critical components of your financial health that can change your life. We'll start with the first four: cash flow, debt, saving, and growth. The fifth and the most important—protection—will follow in a conversation all its own.

PART TWO

CONVERSATIONS TO BUILD YOUR WORTH

Breaking Ground: Four Things That Can Make or Break Your Financial Foundation

As you think about building your financial foundation, consider the five critical components listed below. A qualified financial advocate can guide you through documentation and review them to help you embrace the importance of these five areas. He or she can not only respond to your important questions about these five areas but will thoroughly explain their impacts on your dreams and aspirations.

If you do not have a financial advocate, you can still get started. By reviewing the components below, evaluate your knowledge to determine if a financial advocate could be helpful.

The five components are the following:

1. **Cash Flow:** Are you even aware of what's coming in? What's going out? Where does it all go, and how can you control it? Are there changes you can make to increase your cash flow or adjust your spending plan?

2. **Debt:** Which debt is deductible or good debt? Which debt is considered bad debt? Is there a way to consolidate bad debt or pay it off in a strategic fashion that won't spin out new debt?

3. **Saving:** How can you save enough money to keep you safe and help make your dreams reality? What's the best way to save?

4. **Growth:** Beyond savings, there is the need to grow money for the future. How can you use your money to persistently make *more* money? How should you be thinking of diversifying your money to get the results you want?

5. **Protection:** How can you finally answer the question, "Am I going to be OK?" with a resounding *Yes!* What role does insurance play in my ability to ensure I am going to be financially OK?

Let's look at the first four critical components of your financial health: cash flow, debt, saving, and growth.

ONE: CASH FLOW

Employment or Money In

Money flows in and out of our daily lives. As it flows in and out, it is critical that we focus not on making more but on keeping more. If you spend everything you make, you will always struggle financially. While if you keep more (even from a lesser amount), you will start to build a foundation of security and freedom.

Most of us keep money flowing in though our regular employment, but there are other sources of income as well: bonuses, side hustles or gigs, rental income, stock dividends or profits, royalties, tax refunds, inheritance, trusts, investments, gifts, lottery windfalls, gambling gains, and more.

When getting a new job, there are many decisions that come with it that affect your cash flow. A new job involves decisions around your contract, including benefits such as stock options; various healthcare coverage tiers; and insurance choices like term or permanent life, disability, and voluntary coverage. These benefits can be valuable and shouldn't be discounted. If you have a financial advocate, ask them to guide you through evaluating the real value that these benefits can bring you.

There can be so many additional questions when it comes to money that flows into your coffers: If you inherit or are gifted money, what are the tax implications on your side of the ledger? What about investments: Should you sell stocks and take profits, or will you incur higher taxes by doing so? If you decide to work for yourself, there are even more considerations to evaluate, including how to prevent comingling incoming business funds with other monies and how to protect your personal finances from exposure to business losses. There may be a lot to maneuver, but you can work through it. Ask questions, get clarity, and research what you need to know.

Spending Snapshot or Money Out

The timeworn term *budgeting* can conjure up images of having to give up your favorite avocado toast and coffee drink. Whereas, assessing "money out" constitutes more of a *spending plan that feels more positive and motivating without the judgment or guilt.* Your goal is to simply see where you currently are and what can be eliminated or reduced to allow you to have what is really important (think values and goals).

Google has taught us that you can't get anywhere if you don't know your current location. You can type in that location, or you can even rely on GPS to know where you are. Today, many of us use software apps that use a GPS of sorts to track our daily expenses, even if we don't have time to do it manually. Intuit's Mint.com and PersonalCapital.com are two that come to mind, and they're a lot like GPS for daily spending. Or you can keep a money journal, writing down all the things you spend money on throughout the day. This will help you get clear about where you are and what you value. It has been said that if you want to see what you value, look at what you spend money on. And there's something to be said about actually writing it down yourself. Your money in and money out columns, compared, will tell you almost everything you need to know to get your *Where Am I Now?* exercise going.

> **Ask yourself: Would I give up this yoga class or vacation in Cancun to achieve those dreams?**

Then, create an additional column that pulls out all your monthly *nondiscretionary* spending numbers: rent, utilities, car payments and gas and maintenance, food, internet, and so on—the things you *must* have in life to function. In a final column, list all of your *discretionary* spending: travel, clothing, gifts, donations (unless you consider certain donations nondiscretionary), streaming charges, restaurants, and personal care (hair, gym, etc.).

If you have trouble deciding what is genuine discretionary spending, just turn your thoughts to those things you so fervently want to financially achieve in your life (staking your own business, buying a forever house, moving to Europe, assisting your aging parents), and ask yourself: *Would I give up this yoga class or vacation in Cancun to achieve those dreams?* (When you put it that way, you'll be surprised how many spending items will slide into the "can live without it" category.)

The first point of this exercise is to see *Where You Are Right Now*. In the twenty-first century, with click to purchase, women (like everyone else) can have very little sense of where they are in their daily, weekly, and monthly spending—think no further than your Amazon account. They can wonder why they are not getting any closer to their dreams and aspirations. Yet, women are busy, busy people who may not have had the time to think about assessing their own "money in, money out" snapshot.

The second point of this exercise is to look for the obvious places where you can clean up your financial act. After completing this leg of the process, you may exclaim, "I had no *idea* that I spend $80 a month on streaming services and $400 a month on eating out! That's almost $480 a month or $5,760 a year—the cost of the vacation I've been dying to take!" In fact, discretionary spending cleanup resulted in a condo down payment for a professional millennial who saw owning her own home as an elusive dream. In reality, her dream was within her reach, but she never stopped robotically spending long enough to create her snapshot.

TWO: DEBT

Yes, we certainly discussed good debt and bad debt earlier, but let's take a deeper dive into what these two types of debt may mean specifically to *you*.

Good Debt

Generally, good debt is debt that is *deductible*—a college loan, for instance, or a mortgage. For many, affordable home mortgage debt still makes it worth it to own (instead of rent) a home. Not only do you build up equity but, depending on your tax situation, you may also be able to deduct the interest payments as well. In addition, you can use good debt as a way to maintain control over your capital. If you are debt-free but have no cash on hand, then when you need money, you will either have to incur debt again or be forced to liquidate an asset. By using good debt to help you maintain cash flow outside of that asset, you will have more freedom and flexibility. However, this doesn't mean letting loans, like college loans, sit accruing interest without a plan to pay them off. It means being strategic about how you use debt to maintain control and agility within your entire financial picture.

When women understand how good debt can work for them, they generally see where in their own lives they can take advantage of it. If you are taking out debt to invest in your future, the launch of a business, perhaps, then that debt could be considered good debt. Taking on debt for a business is not the same as debt for personal reasons. You should be willing to invest in your business but do so without using high-interest loans and credit cards. There are business credit cards that can be acquired that have reasonable rates. Check with your credit card provider and your bank for options.

It's all about financial control and using your funds to achieve your unique goals. But, as we discussed early on, these types of decisions rely on a highly personal values assessment, plus having the needed information at one's fingertips. Read the fine print of any loan or credit card documents. Know what you are agreeing to so that there are no surprises. And ask questions until you fully understand the terms.

Bad Debt

Bad debt is credit card, car loan, and similar nondeductible and often high-interest debt. The danger with this type of debt is that it can start a spiraling of events. If you had the cash to make the purchase outright, you would likely not be using a credit card. Therefore, you know that it will take some time to acquire the money to pay off the card. In the meantime, you are incurring more debt because of the increasingly high interest rates.

If you are like many people who pay only the minimum amount each month, then the spiraling gets worse. Many people think they can pay the minimums on these cards for a while and deal with paying them off down the road. By the time "down the road" comes about, the interest rates have caused this debt to become unmanageable and suffocating. Seventy-seven million Americans have debt that is in collections, according to credit report files. Once a debt is in collections, the interest rates can increase even more, making it harder to pay off—especially if you are entering into a later stage in life when retirement or healthcare costs can be looming.[18]

But wait, what about those reward cards? The ones that give you cash back or points for use on flights and hotels? Even these types of cards can be problematic if you continue to keep them maxed out and pay only the minimums. If you want to use these cards (I have a couple myself), then make sure you strive to pay them off consistently each month, and if you can't pay it off, never let the balance exceed 30 percent of the credit limit. These rewards cards can be useful if you travel a great deal or use the points on experiences, but

---

18   Jonnelle Marte, "A Third of Consumers with Credit Files Had Debts in Collections Last Year," *Washington Post*, July 29, 2014, https://www.washingtonpost.com/news/wonk/wp/2014/07/29/a-third-of-consumers-had-debts-in-collections-last-year/?noredirect=on.

you don't want to sacrifice your credit score just for a free trip.

As for creative hacks to keep spending under control, I advise clients to use one or two major credit cards only and resist the temptation to take out high-interest-rate store cards. Store retailers, for instance, are savvy about adding tempting discounts or other incentives to their cards. While these may seem attractive at the point of purchase, long term they can adversely affect your credit rating or feed into unfortunate spending habits.

> **To keep spending under control, I advise clients to use one or two major credit cards only and resist the temptation to take out high-interest-rate store cards.**

For more tips on how to rebuild your credit score, go to sites like www.consumersadvocate.org/credit-repair/reviews for companies that specialize in credit repair. Checking your credit report at least annually is essential to stay on top of mistakes and how your rate changes. Pay bills on time, and be willing to reach out and negotiate better rates with your credit card companies directly.

When it comes to debt, women in particular find themselves in debt quagmires others may not. They may, for instance, struggle to find adequate funding to launch or expand a business, have to take out higher education loans to jump-start careers or augment career paths, or put living expenses on a credit card when their income levels don't rise as anticipated due to a discrepancy in the wage gap. Understand that your credit rating looks at your *reportable income* versus your credit card balances. For example, after a divorce, if your only source of income is nonreportable child support, credit agencies may view your revolving card balances as way out of sync with your income. That means you may encounter serious difficulties qualifying for home and car loans, which could be essential to your survival on your own.

So it's important to assess your spending snapshot and personal life situation *before* acquiring any type of debt, auto, home, business, or academic financing. After you make a well-considered decision, consider putting the loan payment on autopay to ensure the nondiscretionary payment is not jeopardized by out-of-control discretionary spending and to build your credit score by never missing or being late for a loan payment.

THREE: SAVING

In previous chapters, we talked about saving and the importance of having access to money when needed for emergencies, opportunities, or challenges. While building a nest egg for retirement is essential, that should not be considered your *only* source of savings. Many retirement plan vehicles are illiquid and can't be invaded without a tax penalty, except in certain circumstances. Since there is quite a bit of life to lead between where you are today and retirement, having all your money tied up and untouchable creates a challenge. Many times, without a source of savings, when you need money and can't get to it, you end up going into debt or stopping other long-term plans. Therefore, establishing a liberty fund first, before you save for retirement, will set you up for more consistent success along the way.

Conserving hard-earned income through a liquid savings strategy on top of retirement savings is the route to genuine security and can greatly increase inner peace and happiness. Devise any more modern term that is appealing to you, but *save your money*! Without funds in the bank, you can't possibly proceed to the critical and fundamental section that follows.

FOUR: GROWTH

When we think about growing or investing our money, we usually think about our long-term goals, the most typical of which is retirement. When thinking about long-term goals, you have a unique opportunity to take advantage of a critical benefit—time. When you invest for the long term, you can take advantage of a longer period for which your money can grow. But to do that, you must first consider how comfortable you are with risk. Then you should implement a good diversification strategy while maintaining as much control as possible.

Diversification can sound complicated and mysterious if you're not into investing or have never worked with a financial professional. In fact, many people can fail to consider that diversification can take many forms beyond investing in different types of accounts, such as stocks, bonds, and cash. Some other types of diversification can include tax diversification. If, for instance, all your funds are invested in qualified plans for retirement, they're basically in one type of investment for tax purposes. Although you will not pay taxes on those investments until you retire, when you do retire, you'll be concerned about keeping your taxes as low as possible. You may be living largely on Social Security and whatever you are required to draw from your retirement fund every month. You may even have a retirement gig to supplement your retirement income. On top of that, you will no longer have many of your preretirement tax deductions and exemptions for business, mortgage, and children. The result—you may not end up in the low tax bracket you had assumed.

So, if *all* the money you have saved for retirement is tax deferred, that postponed tax hit could deliver quite a surprise. And when you do pay that tax on those retirement accounts, you will likely be paying tax at ordinary income rates. By diversifying in other types of invest-

ANDE FRAZIER

ments outside a qualified retirement plan, you can take advantage of lower capital gains rates, giving yourself options when you need them the most.

You should also consider diversifying based on what you need the money to do. If you desire current income, look for investments that generate income, like bonds or blue-chip stocks that pay dividends regularly. If you are looking for more long-term growth and don't need the money anytime soon, then consider investments that don't pay an income but have a great opportunity to appreciate in value over time. And don't forget real estate as an option. Real estate can provide both income and appreciation while also giving you some tax benefits. The key to real estate is structuring the debt and having liquidity outside the property so you remain in control.

Investment Risk, Comfort, and Access to Funds

If you are working with a financial advocate, they can provide value in terms of how your money aligns with your goals *and* your comfort level. One way many financial advocates are working with women is in the area of socially responsible investing (investing in companies that support the environment, gender equality, or family leave, for instance), if that is important to you.

Knowing your comfort level with regard to risk is essential to long-term success. All too many times, I see people who love it when their investments grow but panic when the market takes a turn southward. Your risk tolerance is your ability to handle fluctuations in the market. And a thorough risk assessment will place you precisely where you should be on the spectrum of risk tolerance, from aggressive growth to risk averse. That tolerance level can change dramatically, depending upon your stage of life and any number of factors, and should be continually reassessed. Again, a good advocate will guide you to create a plan that works for you.

Investing Now and Spending Later

As you begin to approach making decisions for growth, keep in mind that you may have two different stages to plan for: investing money during your working years and spending money in retirement. There are many resources out there that discuss investing money for the future, but at some point, you will need to access those funds to live. When evaluating any recommendations, you should be aware of how you will get to the money when you need it. A well-rounded plan for growth should include an understanding of the endgame.

Clearly, when it comes to financial growth, you can never start your long-range planning too soon, as every decision you make along the way will ultimately affect your comfort and security down the line.

How Well Do You Handle Money In and Money Out?

Check out your cash flow snapshot by seeing how many yes responses you can tick off on the list of seven questions below. You can copy this simple quiz, review it monthly, and use your results as a simple blueprint for modifying your behavior and building great money habits. Make your goal seven yes responses, and you'll be golden!

1. **Financial GPS:** Do you know exactly how much money you have available every month for nondiscretionary and discretionary spending (that is, *net* after paycheck

deductions, auto savings, and other self-instituted with-holding)? YES NO

2. **Dollars available after nondiscretionary spending:** Do you know exactly how much money you will have available for discretionary spending after you have paid all monthly nondiscretionary bills such as rent, food, and utilities? YES NO

3. **Tracking spending:** Do you have a bona fide digital (expense-tracking app) or conventional (running checkbook ledger or pocket-size expense notebook) means of checking your expenditures daily or weekly? YES NO

4. **Checking accounts online:** Do you check the online portal of your bank accounts (or your mobile banking app) for your balance at some time each day? YES NO

5. **Creating or revising spending plan:** Have you recently sat down to devise or revise your monthly budget after reviewing all spending for the past three to six months? YES NO

6. **Overdrafts:** Is your checking or money out account rarely or never overdrawn? (Rarely is once or twice a year.) YES NO

7. **Loss of spending control:** Checking your accounts, are you rarely surprised by an expense you were not antici-pating or an expenditure you forgot you had made? (Rarely is once or twice a year.) YES NO

Feeling Secure: Protecting What You've Built

"Will I be OK?" You may think you are alone is asking this question, but financial planners hear this from their female clients every day— and it's the right question to ask if you care about your financial security. It is also the most important aspect of your financial picture to address, because you can't fix a mistake in the area of protection after the fact.

As we look at all different types of protection, keep in mind that a decision, or lack thereof, in any of these areas can have a tremendous impact on a woman's ability to keep exponentially *expanding and growing* her worth. These areas of protection include various types of insurance, common government benefits, and will or trust documents. Let's start with the one many women have questions about: life insurance.

LIFE INSURANCE: HOW MUCH SHOULD YOU HAVE?

When it comes to life insurance, you should think of answering two questions: (1) how much you should have, and (2) what type you should own.

Most people think that life insurance is solely about providing financial *assistance* in the event of death, but there's much more to it. When it comes to making a decision about how much life insurance you should have, consider what insurance is really designed to do. The definition of insurance is to replace the value of the asset you are insuring. For example, if we were insuring a home, we would consider the value of the home. What would it cost us to replace it in the event of a loss? When considering how much life insurance you should have, first think of the economic value of the person you are insuring. Simply put, an individual's economic worth or economic life value calculates a person's value based on current income and age and multiplies that by the number of years they will most likely be working (to age 65, for example). Other factors like occupation, health, and heredity can also be considered.

By looking at the economic value of one's life, you will be taking a more comprehensive approach to insurance. This approach allows you to cover both specific and unforeseen needs. And covering both these needs is exactly why it is important to separate out the two conversations about life insurance. You first need to know how much you could own, which is based on your economic value, then you can make a decision about type based on affordability. When you collapse the two, you fall into the trap of purchasing insurance based on solving for the baseline of what you think you need. This approach becomes problematic because it is impossible to know what your needs will be over time. You can make good guesses, but with a needs approach, if you are wrong, it could be punitive to your family's future.

When thinking about life insurance, many look at what the insured is earning and what it might be like to suddenly be without that income. They may even consider education costs for children and other large expenses that may be upcoming. However, sellers of insurance policies are not likely to bring up the issue of an individual's earning potential over, say, thirty or forty years, and the fact is that it is likely to increase as people advance in their careers. And few insurance sales reps mention that the cost of living will doubtless increase over the coming decades as well, raising the cost of all expenses.

This shortcoming ends up determining an amount of insurance for an individual that is less than what is really needed if insuring for full value. While many insurance representatives might use various assumptions to help determine the amount of insurance that would actually be needed at the death of the individual, this guesstimate of income needs at some point in the future is risky due to the impossibility of fully knowing what needs will be at any other time than in the present.

When considering the amount of insurance you should own, consider that while you are earning money, you are also saving money for the future. If you are no longer around, not only will current income be lost but all the future savings from that income as well. If you don't fully replace your economic value, your family may find that they cannot save money in the same way because your income was not fully replaced.

In contrast, what is certain is that the economic life value planning approach provides your family with the insurance amount equal to what the income earner would have earned if they had remained alive. This planning gives the best chance for the future that you had originally planned for had you remained alive.

But what about coverage for the one who handles more of the domestic needs or stays home and raises the children? What if that person dies, leaving others to manage without those economic and domestic contributions? How will a life insurance policy help to replace all that this individual contributed? How can that individual's contributions and worth be valued while still alive? Although these are issues for *all* to consider, no matter what their gender makeup, career, or income status, these are certainly issues that women, in particular, so frequently face when considering the purchase of life insurance products.

Though it's admittedly more difficult to forecast a woman's hard-dollar worth as her earning ability is interrupted again and again over the years, it's not difficult to see that an individual caring for other family members has tremendous value. I've lately seen greater consistency among insurance companies as they evaluate such worth: some companies attribute dollar amounts to functions; others rely on the insurance agent and the clients to create and propose a case regarding what it would cost to replace this foundational person.

LIFE INSURANCE: WHAT TYPE SHOULD I OWN?

When it comes to choosing which *type* of life insurance to own, you will want to look at affordability. Affordability, however, should not be determined solely based on the price. You should also look at what the cost of this insurance will be over time, along with other benefits it provides you. Let's look at the two most common types of insurance: term, or temporary, insurance and permanent insurance.

Term insurance is typically described as the most affordable. That's because the premiums an individual pays for term life insurance serve only to provide a death benefit to beneficiaries if that person dies during a specified term (ordinarily ten or fifteen years). Think of it as renting insurance—you can have it for a while, but you don't own it, and it cannot build any type of equity.

On the other hand, permanent life insurance usually does not expire, unlike term insurance, and has two functions. The first is to provide security to a beneficiary in the event of death of the insured. The second is to provide a living value in the form of a savings portion to the insured while they are alive. Both functions of the permanent insurance can provide a valuable resource to all individuals, families, and businesses.

> **Having permanent life insurance in place throughout your retirement can provide you with something extremely valuable: choice.**

Now, what about coverage benefits? Most people think they will need life insurance coverage only while they have a mortgage to be paid and have children living at home who need to be supported. They believe they do not need insurance for a full twenty or thirty years and certainly not when they retire. By then they will have grown their retirement accounts and paid off their mortgages, and their kids will have left the nest.

However, having permanent life insurance in place throughout your retirement years can provide you with something extremely valuable: choice. We have no idea what life will really look like when we retire. We don't know what our health will look like or where we will want to live or if we will have saved enough to not work at all. What we do know is that life will change. Having the ability to use your money in a way that serves you at that point in life is perhaps the most coveted goal of all.

Permanent life insurance can give you the ability to spend the other money you have saved differently. You can make different decisions with your house, your healthcare, your investments, and your family arrangements all based on knowing that if something happens, life insurance will be there to supplement or replace what was spent.

Today, there are countless permanent insurance products and hybrids, all designed to meet varying needs and budgets at different points in life; products change and improve all the time. Young women can start small and keep upgrading and expanding their policies as their incomes increase. If needed, your financial advocate can help evaluate permanent life offerings as the genuine protection products they are, designed to provide all sorts of flexibility along the way.[19]

Six Unsung Benefits of Permanent Life Insurance

Beyond the outstanding protection qualities, permanent life insurance offers these benefits:

1. **Builds a savings element (typically known as cash value)** that you can borrow against or surrender a portion of for needed funds. This serves as an indispensable tool for guaranteeing financial and life options when they are most needed for emergencies, such as a debilitating illness (especially if no long-term-care insurance is held)

---

19 Policies may be customized to the needs of policyholders in endless ways: death benefits may be distributed precisely as stipulated by the policyholder, for instance. Another helpful option is a waiver of premium benefit, which allows premiums to be paid *for* the policyholder should he or she become disabled or unable to pay.

or for once-in-a-lifetime business opportunities.

2. **The cash value accumulated can be obtained** without filling out forms, needing to be gainfully employed, or waiting for a credit check to clear.

3. **There is no repayment schedule or requirement for monies borrowed.** (Note: The amount owed will be reduced from the death benefit. Always pay the loan interest on any loans taken from cash value, as not repaying the amount could cause the policy to lapse.)

4. **In most states, a permanent life policy cannot be attacked by creditors.**

Although term insurance may have a helpful place in a woman's protection portfolio, permanent life protection can provide the freedom to take educated risks to optimize money in life-changing ways. A discussion with a qualified permanent life insurance agent can be eye opening. Your agent should represent a reputable permanent life carrier with high industry (AM Best and Moody's) ratings and should offer a no-obligation consultation, during which you can ensure rapport and probe to see if your philosophies are aligned.

The agent should routinely work with female clients and fully understand women's financial issues, such as the prevalence of interrupted earning histories and longevity concerns. Whether you look for a knowledgeable independent agent (representing multiple companies) or a "captive" agent (one who has long and deep experience with a single company), aim to locate a representative who is always learning and is passionate about creating insurance solutions for their clients.

Once you have evaluated your life insurance, then you will want to align that with your will, trust documents, and advanced directives.

WILLS AND TRUSTS: ADVANCE DIRECTIVES AND HEALTHCARE PROXIES

Advanced directives are legal documents that enable you to spell out your decisions about end-of-life care in advance in order to avoid confusion down the line, communicating your wishes to family, friends, and healthcare professionals. Some of the more common ones include the following:

- **A living will** outlines which care you want if you are dying or permanently unconscious. You can choose to have care or refuse it—the choice is yours—but you have to indicate your preferences.

- **A heathcare proxy**—The person you choose to make sure your wishes are carried out if you are not able. This person should be someone you trust and is comfortable making decisions based on your wishes. Combine this with a durable power of attorney for healthcare, which is the document needed to state whom you choose to be your healthcare proxy.

- **A do not resuscitate order**—This order will instruct the medical staff treating you on whether you want to be resuscitated. This is more commonly used with older patients and those with terminal illnesses.

Not sure why you would need advance directives or healthcare proxies? The reasons are many:

- **Establish advance directives that indicate who would have the right to make decisions for you (power of attorney)** in the event that you are incapacitated and cannot make medical and related decisions for yourself. This is important even if you are young and have no assets or children.

- **There are various levels of healthcare proxy you can include in advance directives,** plus a living will and a do not resuscitate order that will allow others to carry out your end-of-life or medically related wishes (they vary from state to state). (For helpful online resources, see exhibit 2 in the resources section at the back of the book.)

- **Directives can cover myriad issues** such as tissue and organ donation, resuscitation and life support, Alzheimer's disease, and psychiatric or other conditions that affect the ability to communicate your wishes.

- **A living will details which types of medical treatments an individual would or would not want** in the above situations. It can also describe under which specific conditions prolonging life should be started or stopped. (Legal requirements for living wills vary from state to state.)

- **Discuss your wishes with loved ones before you sign!** Even placing "organ donor" on your driver's license could be a surprise at a difficult moment, if not discussed beforehand. If you are about to be married, discussions about advance directives could lead you and your fiancé into essential conversations about life values and money management (more about this in the next chapter).

Wills and Trusts

When it comes to wills, women often assume they will not die anytime soon, don't have much in the way of assets, and therefore don't need to draw up such a document. The decision gets put to the back of the list as life proceeds to "happen." The question is: Do you want the state to decide where your assets will go? Or leave it up to someone else to decide?

> The question is: Do you want the state to decide where your assets will go?

Understanding how wills and trusts function can help you protect your heirs by ensuring certain monies avoid probate. (Every state has different ways of handling this.) Other aspects of your life and estate must also be carefully considered, including children from previous marriages; your intention to bequeath assets such as art, jewelry, cars, or sentimental items to charities or specific individuals; and final preferences such as cremation versus burial. Attach these wishes to your will, and discuss them with your loved ones so that everyone is aware of them. If desired, your personal financial advocate can ease the process.

Importantly, you need to determine guardians and alternate guardians of your minor children if something should happen to you. To avoid the apprehension of financial burden, also indicate how you will allocate funds to the guardians to care for the children. The allocation of funds for guardianship must be carefully designed so you can ensure your children are truly taken care of in the manner you would have wanted. Guardianship decisions need to be approved by all potential guardians beforehand and revisited over the years as interpersonal relationships change and people relocate. Your children's happiness and well-being is not something you would want to leave to the state or to be determined in a family squabble.

Surprisingly, even people with sizable assets and large families can be delinquent in their responsibilities to their loved ones. The Queen of Soul, Aretha Franklin, was one of the most celebrated female artists in recent times, yet when it came to her estate, it was discovered that she had several handwritten wills and had neglected to create a trust. This has resulted in a complicated dispute over her estate's control.

When assets are involved, the creation of wills and especially trusts is best left to the guidance of a very capable estate attorney. You can locate a qualified professional with extensive experience by asking for a referral from other trusted team professionals or individuals you trust. Interview potential legal advisors during a brief no-charge consultation and come prepared with information the attorney might require to assess your situation. Estate attorneys may specialize, which can be very helpful to you—an eldercare estate attorney, for instance, would be beneficial if you are revising your will at retirement age or helping an older family member. Understand that trusts are not only for the wealthy; they are simply instruments designed to protect assets for heirs by taking full advantage of federal and state tax laws instated to provide such protection.

If you have limited assets, no children, and do not wish to use the services of an estate attorney, you can devise a simple will via an online will form or template (google "will form" for endless resources), or a hard copy form is available from stationery and office supply stores. Add an attachment that covers your last wishes regarding burial versus cremation plus the disbursement of favorite items. Make sure the will is signed and witnessed as directed; notarizing witnesses' signatures will eliminate the need for their testimony in probate court. (A holographic or handwritten will may not be legal in your state; check before devising your will this way.) Retain the original copy of your will for yourself and send copies to your attorney, financial advocate (if you have one), and those close to you, or it may be assumed that no will exists. Revisit your will or trusts and accessory documents whenever any major life change occurs, such as marriage, divorce, relocation, childbirth, and significant health changes. Otherwise, revisit and review essential documents every five years. Again, a financial advocate, along with a good attorney, can help ensure your process is solid.

HEALTH INSURANCE

The most important thing here is to assess health insurance and other employment benefits *before* you decide to accept a new job, launch your own business, become self-employed, or work as a digital nomad. You may also need to decide whether it would be wiser to pursue a single full-time position with benefits as opposed to taking on a part-time nonbenefits job or side gig. Although there are tax considerations, employer-subsidized health insurance can represent what might otherwise be huge dollar amounts in self-paid premiums, not to mention a vast difference in coverage should you be responsible for paying for

> **Assess health insurance and other employment benefits *before* you decide to accept a new job, launch your own business, become self-employed, or work as a digital nomad.**

your own health insurance. Your question should be: How will your healthcare insurance protect *both* your health and finances from potential devastation?

Women can assume their health will remain stable in their twenties or thirties, but that is not always the case, and even small health issues, procedures, and ER visits can be costly.[20] Then, too, in the United States, childbirth costs have tripled since the late '90s—just another reason why the most recent generation of women and their partners have delayed having children until their finances improve.

There are also significant healthcare benefit issues to weigh if you wish to launch your own business with employees who will be comparing benefits in your industry. Once again, your financial team can help you make decisions that will help your business compete in its marketplace.

DISABILITY AND LONG-TERM-CARE INSURANCE

When women want to know "Will I be OK?" they are not only asking, in effect, "Who will take care of me if I become ill or disabled?" They often mean, "Could I end up on the street or have to go to family members for help?" These fears are very real for both wholly independent women and even for women in long-term relationships with partners who have managed their financial affairs. Almost everyone has heard of someone left destitute or dependent on others.

Earlier in this book, we talked about long-term-care insurance: how women are more likely to make sure they're covered, while men

---

20 "How Much Does an Emergency Room Visit Cost?" CostHelper Health, accessed November 12, 2019, https://health.costhelper.com/emergency-room.html. Emergency room visits in 2019 cost up to $3,000 without health insurance.

often assume that somebody else will take care of them. If you have a personal financial advocate, by all means discuss *very early on* how to plan for your care and financial protection in the event of illness and disability. There are many ways to achieve such protection. Securing it early, at affordable rates, can make all the difference.

Even today, women often assume that their Social Security benefits or employer-paid disability insurance will resolve a sudden inability to support oneself. In most cases, however, any such benefits fall short of real-life need. Disability coverage may not begin for a period of months after a triggering event, during which time you could find your life in upheaval while you are least able to cope and most likely to make the quickest, ill-advised decisions.

Long-term-care insurance is an excellent protection option if purchased early enough for premiums to be affordable throughout your lifetime. There are myriad options for all levels of care, including in-home care. Many women who have battled chronic illnesses such as diabetes, autoimmune, and other conditions wisely acknowledge that, should those conditions worsen, they would want care that allows them to continue their lives with as little disruption as possible to themselves and their loved ones.

Yet there are other routes to lifetime protection for disability and the care you might need for a chronic or debilitating illness. Permanent life insurance can provide an excellent option, as there are many features within this type of insurance that can provide access to additional resources if needed. A personal financial advocate should be able to discuss these types of creative alternatives. The operative message here is: put together a solid plan and do it *early*.

SOCIAL SECURITY BENEFITS

Many important issues about Social Security benefits don't crop up until women are nearing the age of retirement. They then look back on their lives and note all the things they would have done differently if only they had known better.

Keesha and her husband, Rick, for instance, had their own company, but for years, to show a profit on the books, the business did not pay Keesha a salary for her work. That was great for the company but, as it turned out, bad for Keesha. Since she showed no income for those years, she also had no Social Security benefits reflecting her work. Her best option at that point was to collect benefits on her husband's income, but had she paid into Social Security, she may have found she could have received higher benefits.

During the years that Ashley stayed home to raise and homeschool her four children, her husband, Jordan, was racking up Social Security benefits as a full-time employee of an energy company. But Ashley was considered an unpaid worker, even though she taught four students for six hours every day. The financial advocate she finally chose suggested she become employed by a homeschooling company to teach her four kids and two other local children, thus continuing to earn income and Social Security benefits as well. Ashley may continue as a homeschooler, even after her own children move on to college.

Social Security is ever changing, and for many, there is concern about what will even be available when they get to retirement age. Regardless of where you are on this journey, your best plan is to ask questions and know your options. You can go to the US Social

Security Administration website[21] to access your Social Security account, learn all you can about various benefits, and keep on top of your own protection picture.

HOMEOWNERS AND AUTO INSURANCE

Homeowners and auto insurance coverage are essential for a protected life. Because there are so many critical issues to assess within each type of coverage, it's vital to have the best possible referrals to the most qualified representatives of top-rated insurers. Cheap insurance should not be your goal, for it is usually *solely* that: cheap.

What you need most is *value* in your homeowners and car coverage, balancing the quality of protection with what you can afford. Many people believe that they are on their own when it comes to researching carriers and green-lighting agent proposals. Not so when you work with an advocate who can review all current policies and coverage, suggest coverage improvement if necessary, and—most importantly— make certain that there are no coverage gaps anywhere that could leave you vulnerable to financial calamity, legal action, and personal hazard. Even car insurance can keep other assets protected in the event of an auto injury claim that might otherwise be devastating.

---

21   US Social Security Administration, https://www.ssa.gov. The US Social Security Administration website offers a full range of information about benefits but is not designed to acquaint the public with specialized information about navigating and optimizing the system. Work with your certified financial planner or certified Social Security benefits specialist to avail yourself of important opportunities.

How Well Am I Protected?

To gauge where you (and your mate, if applicable) stand right now vis-à-vis your financial, life, and health protection, see how many yes responses you can tick off on the list of questions below, after having read through the previous chapter. Then use your no responses in this quiz as your starting-gate tick list to secure appropriate protection.

1. **Life Insurance:** I am satisfied that I am fully protected by the best life insurance coverage possible, providing the most value and with a coverage strategy for the future. YES NO

2. **Advance Directives (living wills, healthcare proxies, personal wishes, etc.):** After a thoughtful discussion of preferences and personal wishes, I have thoroughly reviewed all my advance directives for the state in which I reside. YES NO

3. **Wills and Trust Agreements:** I have thoroughly reviewed all of my wills and/or trust agreements for the state in which I reside and have communicated my desires to important family members. YES NO

4. **Health Insurance:** I am satisfied that I am fully protected by the best healthcare coverage possible, providing the most value for the investment that can currently be made and with a coverage strategy for the future. YES NO

5. **Social Security Benefits:** I have a solid understanding of how Social Security benefits work, have reviewed my

current benefit status, and am satisfied that I am or will be maximizing the benefits available to me. YES NO

6. **Disability and/or Long-Term-Care Insurance:** I have a solid understanding of how both disability and long-term-care insurance coverages work. I have coverage in place at present or am consulting a qualified professional about acquiring the most effective coverage (or using an equivalent strategy) in the near future. YES NO

7. **Homeowners and Auto Liability Insurance:** I am either fully covered by reputable carriers of the above insurance products or will be consulting a qualified professional about acquiring the most effective coverage in the near future. (Business liability insurance may or may not be applicable.) YES NO

Love and Money: How Relationships Can Either Solidify or Shatter Your Financial Foundation

Women often do not think deeply about their financial safety when they fall in love and marry. They assume that the love they share with their partner will protect them from hardship or, at the very least, help them through tough financial times. But it doesn't always work out that way, does it?[22]

---

22   "1 In 5 Women Experience Post-Divorce Poverty," Law Corner, August 16, 2019, https://www.thelawcorner.com/1-5-women-experience-post-divorce-poverty/. One In five women fall into poverty after divorce.

IF ONLY THEY HAD TALKED ABOUT MONEY

Danielle and Jake began dating just around the time she began to work with an advisor on her financial plan. Before Danielle could fully commit to Jake, she wanted to know more about his attitude toward money and finances; his financial behavior and beliefs were important to her. She saw that he wore nice clothes, traveled, took good care of his car, and had no trouble paying for dates, but she had no idea if he had a mature attitude about money.

Her advisor suggested that visiting his parents would tell her a good deal—where he was raised, what his parents were like, how they lived, how they seemed to relate to their son. Later on, she and Jake would be able to speak more frankly about their own money values, and Danielle could find out if their views meshed. When she visited Jake's family, she found that everything looked pretty normal. Yet, as the months went on, Danielle was not able to bring up the awkward conversation about finances. She was afraid that if she brought up the subject, Jake might think she was overly interested in his money.

A few months after their wedding, Danielle finally felt comfortable bringing up the topic of family finances. Should they maintain separate accounts and divide the responsibilities or combine accounts and bill paying? Jake wanted to maintain an account of his own but agreed to set up a joint bill-pay account to which they'd both contribute. Danielle would pay the couple's bills from that account.

Months later, Danielle noticed a charge for a postal service store on a credit card statement, and when she asked Jake about it, he told her it was a mailbox he had neglected to close. He promised to take care of it, but the charge kept recurring. Eventually, Danielle went to the postal store to find out how to close the account. When the store employee handed her the remaining mail, she noticed the envelopes were credit card bills. Later, when she gave them to Jake, he was furious that she had invaded his privacy.

Danielle's advisor then explained that she would need to know about those bills, for they could eventually become a *joint* responsibility. "Is he having an affair?" Danielle wondered aloud. More likely it was credit card debt, her advisor told her. A visit to the mortgage officer at Danielle's bank revealed that while her credit score was 750, Jake's was a dismal 560. What's more, he had $40,000 of credit card debt he had never revealed to her. Then again, she hadn't asked.

> What's more, he had $40,000 of credit card debt he had never revealed to her. Then again, she hadn't asked.

Arguing ensued. Jake got defensive and wouldn't discuss the problems; Danielle became resentful, then stepped in as the fixer to take over management of the debt when Jake wouldn't work on his spending behavior issues. But the minute she paid down some of the debt, Jake would spend again.

Four years after they married, Danielle and Jake were divorced. Danielle had to shoulder 25 percent of Jake's debt and pay an additional $13,000 toward his back taxes to get out of the marriage and get on with her life. Fortunately, there were no children at risk. But both Danielle and Jake had lost precious time—she in her quest to make a happy and stable marriage and start a family, he in any attempt to straighten out his finances and build a life with a mate.

It took Danielle seven or eight years to get her finances and credit back on track. She did marry again, but this time, she found the courage to have the difficult financial conversation early in the relationship. Her new husband told her he was glad she had, since they were both in their midthirties and would need to be financially stable if they wanted children.

How different might Jake and Danielle's story have been if the two had been able to conduct an early conversation about their markedly different financial viewpoints and issues?

MANY WAYS TO MESS UP LOVE AND MONEY

As it stands, there are *endless* ways in which a couple's financial viewpoints and values might differ and thus might damage or doom their relationship. Take Amy, an attractive but financially immature woman drawn only to men with wealth. Amy finally married her millionaire who, early on, treated her like his princess and showered her with expensive clothes and cars. A few years down the line, Amy realized she wasn't exactly a princess but more like the property of a wealthy and controlling man. She had no career, pursued no passions of her own, and had little say in where they went and what they did.[23] "I gave up my life to drive a Range Rover," Amy finally admitted. She and her husband had never discussed their feelings about money and its impact on life. If they had, they each might have realized they were gazing at each other through different eyes and making wholly different bargains.

---

23 Many women don't buy in to their domestic financial "bargain." They suffer under domestic financial abuse, which may or may not be related to domestic violence as well. Yet there are financially narcissistic women, too, who devastate their spouses' finances and then move on to their next mark. Find out more about the signs of financial abuse at https://www.myworthfinance.com/stories/financial-domestic-abuse-what-is-it-and-how-can-we-stop-it/.

The Power to Speak Up for Your Needs

As CEO of myWorth, I hear too many women bemoan the fact that they trusted a soon-to-be ex-husband with their finances. It often turns out that they were simply hesitant to pose questions, ask to see family financial documents, or review what their spouses put before them to sign. But hesitancy can be harmful if it means you don't speak up for your needs!

Sooner or later, I have to ask, "Why were you so willing to *relinquish your financial rights to someone else*, even someone you hoped had your best interest at heart?" I have to point out that when a woman willingly gives away her rights, she must also accept the responsibility for the loss of her financial security.

Be honest with yourself: Are you letting someone else handle the finances because it's easier not to speak up, or are you uncomfortable with admitting you haven't taken the time to learn what you need to in order to make these decisions?

There is no excuse not to take ownership of your financial situation. Awareness is the first step. Now that you're aware, why not start a conversation? Your future depends on it!

MORE THAN MATH BUT PART OF LOVE

If you're not talking about your finances with each other, it's possible you're not talking about your *life* together. You may even be masking critical issues. For example, while money can purchase independence for one partner in a relationship, money can be a means of control to the other. And that's only one example of the myriad ways people differ when it comes to money.

> While money can purchase independence for one partner in a relationship, money can be a means of control to the other.

Have you ever heard someone insist that their breakup was "all about the money"? It's important to keep in mind that as long as people are human beings, it's never just about the money. It's about what the money *represents* or forces to the surface: insecurity, inadequacy, secrecy, an inability to share or be open—any number of very human emotions and traits that are behind markedly different money maxims.

HOW TO START THE CONVERSATION

Launching the discussion any way you can is certainly preferable to never launching it at all. Clearly, it takes courage to bring up a subject as touchy as money. That doesn't mean that you have to jump in with, "Hey, I've been meaning to ask you: How much money do you have anyway?"

Easing in with a logical approach is always a good idea. Something like, "We're beginning to get to know each other, and the one thing so many people don't talk about when they're getting to know each other is money. Let's talk a little bit about it and how we feel about it." Remember, too, not to just listen but to *observe* (even as love may try to blind you!). For instance, how does your new love interest live? What does their spending style appear to be? If you meet their family, how do they live? How do the family members relate to each other when it comes to spending or frugality?

The conversation may even arise organically as you share your views on so many other things: your childhoods, your dreams, your goals. If you are listening carefully to the other person, it may feel quite natural to ask, "You said you were raised in a blue-collar neighborhood, but you had a great education and ended up with a white-collar career. How did your early upbringing affect your views on money? What are your beliefs today about money and finances?" You might even introduce your own similarly relatable story first. And if you have discussed your preferences around having children, this is also a great time to bring up your own feelings about raising children and ask about whether having one person stay at home while the other is working makes sense. If so, how would finances intersect with their views and with yours?

At a certain point in the relationship, as you are both naturally trying to find out about each other, you can certainly mention that talking about money would be helpful to *you*: "I know it may not be a common discussion and may even seem a little uncomfortable, but it would be so helpful to me as we are getting to know each other. Even when styles are different, people can always work toward common ground if they discuss things. What do you think about that?"

> A man is often *relieved* that he has been asked to speak honestly about his views on money.

In my experience, a man is often *relieved* that he has been asked to speak honestly about his views on money. He may have been working hard to impress a woman with his boundless generosity, while, at the same time, he may be worried that any woman he ends up with will give up her own job and rely solely on him. Hearing from a desirable woman that she enjoys going out and loves his generous gifts but *also* cares a great deal about saving money, financially planning for a family and a future, and keeping her own career may be the icing on the cake. If he is concerned that his date is digging to uncover his worth, he may suggest she talk about her own views first. So a woman should certainly make sure she is up to speed about her *own* financial picture before she brings up the topic of *his* finances for discussion.

If a man refuses to have a conversation about money with a woman he is seriously dating, I'd take that as a red flag—there's something going on that he doesn't want you to know about. But if it turns out that *he* is the one who believes in saving, security, and protection, and *you* are more in the mindset of YOLO, then it's a darn good thing you both are discovering that early on.

The point is *everyone* has a story about money. What's yours? What's his? Will they mesh?

Why Won't You Start the Money Conversation? Seven Arguments You Can Beat

Having trouble bringing up the subject of money so that you both can compare your financial styles and beliefs? Check these common underlying barriers—and their solutions.

1. **It's embarrassing to bring up a topic as crass as money.** Consider synonyms for "crass": insensitive, blundering, or vulgar. Caring about your partner's feelings regarding

their hard-earned money means you are *sensitive*, not insensitive! And so what if you blunder a bit? In a relationship *everyone* blunders at some time or another. As for appearing vulgar, you can certainly trust your partner to know your true inner qualities. And if not—well that may be for another discussion.

2. **My partner will think I'm a gold digger only after their bank account.** Only one way to put that issue to rest: tell your mate this isn't about their bank balance; it's about their *style and beliefs* regarding their handling of money. Do they like to save money, grow it, spend it, or a combination of all three? Let them know you're interested in how your styles will mesh, not how much they have in their 401(k). You're not telling them how much you have stashed away either—at least not right now.

3. **Talking about money is unfeminine and will ruin my mystique.** A woman today can run a business, drive a truck, even lead a nation—all while raising children, making a comfortable home, and charming her mate. That IS a woman's mystique, and it makes us perpetually fascinating. We own that!

4. **I'm not ready to move our romantic relationship to such a mundane plane.** As relationships move forward, they need to include reality checks to survive. In fact, experts explain that romantic love needs to evolve into reality-based love to be strong and enduring. "Allowing oneself to be known and at the same time accepting

another person 'as is' can create a deep meaningful connection," according to *Psychology Today*.[24]

5. **We're from different worlds with different obligations, but my partner will come around later on.** Are you deferring your six-figure student loan debt? Do you have aging parents who are planning to live with you and your mate one day? Do you know your guy or gal wants a modest $15,000 wedding while you're envisioning an event for $300,000 plus a gown in the $10k range? Watch out: *you* are the couple who most needs a transparent conversation early on to avert the disaster of surprise.[25]

6. **I don't know what to say! Can I have an advisor there to help me?** If you are concerned that your mate may feel blindsided by you, he or she may be even more uncomfortable in front of your financial advocate. But that doesn't mean *you* can't get valuable guidance from your advocate first. Then choose your approach, jot it down, and practice it until you feel more comfortable. If you begin the conversation and they would *prefer* to discuss financial matters with a professional, by all means

---

24 Ann Smith, "The Reality of Love," *Psychology Today*, December 10, 2010. https://www.psychologytoday.com/us/blog/healthy-connections/201012/the-reality-love.

25 I am reminded of the story about the man who was near death and was visited first by God, then by the devil. God gave the man a sneak peek of heaven to show him the peace and serenity awaiting. The devil then toured him through scenes of revelers partying amid fabulous excess. The man of course chose the underworld as his final destination—so much more fun. Then he died and was greeted by the devil at the gates of hell. Fires raged about him as the man gagged on the stench of brimstone. "Wait a second!" he cried. "This isn't what you showed me!" To which the devil laughed and responded, "Then, you were a prospect. Now, you're a client."

invite a neutral but holistic, goal-oriented financial professional to join in. (This is more likely at the engaged stage, not two months into the relationship.)

7. **We've been married for years, but my partner handles the money, and I've never asked to discuss our finances.** Since you are reading this book, you probably *want* to get involved, and it's never too late. A good opener would be, "I'd really like to learn more about what's going on with our finances so I can take a more active role in managing our finances together. I've never even looked at our insurance policies or our IRA." Then make sure the conversation eventually moves to other documentation, account passwords, and whatever else you will need to know to intervene quickly should you have to. If your mate insists that you don't need to know anything or wants to change will beneficiaries but won't show you the paperwork, be suspicious. Review recent joint tax returns[26] and seek advice.

---

26 Women who file taxes jointly with their spouses are, with very limited exceptions, equally responsible for the veracity of all information included in the returns. Do not sign a joint tax return until you have carefully reviewed it and asked any and all pertinent questions. If your mate cannot answer your questions, review the return with your personal financial advocate *before* signing. And always keep a separate copy of joint tax returns for your own personal files. If a family or marital crisis should occur, you and your advisors will need easy access to that financial information.

A New Legacy: Laying the Groundwork for Your Family's Financial Future

Whether or not we plan to, we teach our children not only about life but about money. *How* we teach them—and *what* we teach them—should not be haphazard but well considered if we want the best for the young people we send into the world with our most profound hopes for happy lives. Denis Waitley, author of *Seeds of Greatness*, crystallized sage (and age-old) advice well when he stated, "The greatest gifts you can give your children are the roots of responsibility and the wings of independence."

Instilling those values is something all parents need to think about early on, rather than later. (And later creeps up way too fast.) This is especially important for a parent—often the female parent—who performs most of the child-rearing duties and thus spends the larger amount of daily or weekly time with the children. Ideally, both parents would be equal influencers because they have come to have similar values about managing money or have worked to create—and live by—a common message for their children. This is not always easy to accomplish, but it's certainly easier when it is a goal. It's harder to look back and wish the discussions had taken place.

Michelle and Chris are the loving parents of Madison, eighteen, and Josh, fifteen. Both parents have worked hard for the family's wonderful home and lifestyle in an affluent neighborhood. And both have tried hard not to fall into traps like buying new cars for their kids.

Yet Michelle admits that entitlement can be a problem. "It's the little things," she says, pointing to the fact that her kids assume that they can order out food whenever they like and put it on a credit card, take an Uber instead of mass transportation, or shop online when it suits them.

Michelle wanted Madison to get a summer job and learn to pay for her own little luxuries just as she did at the same age. But Madison has her heart set on traveling to Europe with friends and doesn't feel the need to work before she "has" to. Josh, too, has plans to go camping with his buddies over the break. So Chris and Michelle will subsidize both of their children's summer plans as they always have.

They want their children to enjoy their young lives, but Michelle and Chris worry that their kids will be unprepared for the coming responsibilities of grown-up daily living if they don't start to practice fiscal responsibility now. Both parents are proud they've been able to give their children so many things they never had themselves. But now they're also looking back with new appreciation at their *own* parents' value systems regarding money. Says Michelle, "My father told me to get a summer job if I wanted to buy my own things. So I did, and I never valued anything quite as much as those first 'big' items I bought. I was so proud of myself. It was great."

INFLUENCING YOUR CHILDREN, ON PURPOSE OR NOT

It may be hard to accept in twenty-first century America, but parents who automatically provide everything for their children all through their lives at home and during college can do their children a great disservice. That's because a child's developmental need to *be provided for* would more naturally evolve toward *providing for oneself* as he or she progresses through the growing-up years.

With their helicopter parenting, Michelle and Chris may have inadvertently been robbing their children of their need to learn to provide for themselves. Like so many well-intentioned parents, Michelle and Chris did not examine their own behavior and ask themselves, If we are indeed overproviding and overprotecting our children from failure or pain, who are we doing it for if it will not benefit our kids? Is it possible we are doing it for *us*?

OUTSIDE INFLUENCES

When our parents and their parents grew up, they were taught at home "a penny saved is a penny earned," and, likely, they were shown how to keep a running balance in a checkbook and double-check their savings passbook at the local bank branch each week. Our modern credit-based society has changed much of that. And what the advent of plastic did not change, the internet did.

Most parents today acknowledge the modern societal influences they must counter daily to keep their children from drowning in instant gratification or complaining that "everyone else has it; why can't I?" Schoolmates, television, cyberspace, and our celebrity-focused culture bombard our children at every juncture, making it hard to deprive them of the endless things that others have. These circumstances make it difficult but not impossible to teach children about the intersections of life and money.

Yet many parents today want to be their children's friend—not necessarily a strong parent. As wonderful as being a BFF is, we are still the primary life guides our children have. We need to effectively guide our children through financial pitfalls that may loom ahead. Importantly, we need to ensure that we teach our daughters about money the same way we teach our sons. And we must impart to our children the earning, spending, and saving skills that will help them adroitly navigate the many unexpected *and* expected life events that could trip them up along the way.

> **We need to ensure that we teach our daughters about money the same way we teach our sons.**

INTERSECTIONS OF LIFE AND MONEY: PRICELESS LESSONS

There are so many nuances of life that can provide a valuable financial learning ground for children. In recent years, experts have been taking a new look at how children develop their life habits, including those of managing money.[27]

---

27   David Whitebread and Sue Bingham, "Habit Formation and Learning in Young Children," The Money Advice Service, May 2013, https://mascdn.azureedge.net/cms/the-money-advice-service-habit-formation-and-learning-in-young-children-may2013.pdf.

Time

When children are very young, that's when parents often introduce the piggy bank and the idea of saving money. That's all well and good, but an even more important lesson for young children is the concept of *waiting*: developing the discipline (and joy) of waiting with great anticipation for something they really want. Developing this skill accomplishes so many things—it

- teaches a child the life skill of waiting;

- teaches a child to work on something that is worth working toward;

- diminishes the often-damaging impact of instant gratification;

- imbues certain dreams and aspirations with a level of joy; and

- provides a pathway to pride in oneself.

Chores

For decades, a parental conundrum has revolved around chores and money. Some parents start early, paying their children to do basic chores at home so that their children experience work and saving as they will in later life: you do a job, you get paid, you put your money in the bank.

Other parents feel it's important to teach children to understand that helping with chores such as making their beds, cleaning their rooms, helping to set the table for dinner, and taking out the trash is part of being a family. (Larger, elective chores such as cleaning out a garage or weeding the lawn are open for compensation.) In some families, children come to learn that daily family tasks are an important part of life, whether in assisting their own family, their community family, or the family of mankind as a whole. We'd all like to know that if our child noticed a neighbor struggling with packages or a heavy trash can, she would step up to assist without ever expecting payment for the effort.

Instilling a sense of family duty does not mean that parents don't need to find ways to *motivate* their children to help around the house or tackle their own personal chores. Often that motivation can amount to sharing your personal values. No matter what your strategic decision—pay for chores or don't pay for chores—always explain your approach, and then be consistent.

Allowance

Just as with the issue of their children's chores, the decision parents make about allowance is a highly personal one. Some parents feel that to teach children the connection between working and saving for the future, the piggy bank or child's saving account should be a receptacle for well-earned payments for family chores, other work around the house, and even first jobs within the community. Some encourage their children to develop the saving habit by banking monetary gifts from family and friends. Other parents happily take their youngsters shopping for a special reward to teach them the joy of saving for a longed-for item. Still other parents see a regular allowance as a young person's right. There's no right or wrong answer. Just remember that what you teach your children about their spending money will greatly influence their *adult* spending attitudes—so

- be clear and consistent about your underlying belief system regarding money and allowances; and

- be ready to course correct not only what *you* were taught about money but what you teach your children, if you see that good money management habits are not taking root.

If your belief system changes due to circumstances (a change in income status, for example), seize the opportunity to *gently* teach children that life changes too. Kristen, who raised her family alone after a financially devastating divorce, thoughtfully explained to her two children that she would have *loved* to give them a weekly allowance, but life just hadn't cooperated with her original plan. So she suggested that they have a family huddle each week to decide what they would do with whatever money they had available to spend or save, even if it was five or ten dollars. And she saved her daily change to distribute each evening. (Her son later used his years of saved change to open an investment account.)

Some weeks, they decided to save for her daughter's much-needed party dress or her son's new bicycle tires. Other weeks, they put the money toward a family car trip or decided to save it for something more important down the line. The children even learned to swap their belongings at the local thrift shop so that they could experience new toys or clothes while their own were repurposed. (Many women today routinely rent designer handbags, dresses, and gowns instead of investing huge sums in infrequently worn items; discussing this strategy with the family can help everyone emulate the same common-sense behavior.)

Kristen's son and daughter were six and ten, respectively, when their mother divorced, but they learned early the art of having family conversations about money. Because the family routinely discussed life, values, and the role of money, the children learned that their financial state at any particular time was not *who* they were and did not define their value as human beings. They also learned that money and material things are not entitlements but life's rewards for effort and thoughtful allocation; they even knew it was important to prepare for unexpected or adverse happenstances.

Even though Kristen's finances improved markedly as her career advanced, her belief system did not change. Her children grew up to be successful adults who could effectively choose when to be frugal, when to recycle, and when to enjoy their good fortune through purchasing something new.

HOW TO START THE CONVERSATION ABOUT FINANCIAL RESPONSE-ABILITY

Can you talk about money with children—even small children? Yes, you can; the scope and context starts small, that's all, and expands as the years move forward. It's all about endowing your children with the ability to respond well to what life may throw at them. That's "response-ability," and *if you model it*, it will prevent them from ignoring and denying life's challenges, floundering, or, at worst, sinking. It will teach them to accept life as it actually is and calmly and confidently attack a problem one step at a time.

I once saw a mother and her five-year-old son wandering down a toy store aisle, considering affordable options. He suddenly pointed to an expensive item and asked, "Mom! Can we get that?" to which she responded, "Not right now, honey, but maybe for Christmas." "Oh, OK," he said, and they walked on. A woman nearby asked, "How did you *do* that?" and the mom explained she had taught her child that *wanting* something is not always a reason for *having* something. People want things all the time, but that doesn't always mean they should spend hard-earned money to buy them.

At five, a child certainly cannot grasp all the adult implications behind his spending conversations with his mother. But he and his parents can donate toys to the local family shelter and shop together at the supermarket, comparing cereal values (more flakes for less money). Such activities help a young person learn about money and about how the grown-up world works. Additionally, the discussion about life and its intersections with saving and spending should be a constant, fluid conversation, not an occasional lecture.

The point here is that *whatever* a parent tells her child will help to set the behavior that child will adopt in life, at least until he or she is old enough to decide to integrate that behavior or change it. The important thing is to give your children the benefit of helpful life skills. Even if your kids are in their teens, you can send them to the grocery store to do the weekly food shopping and let them learn through trial and error how to work with a weekly grocery budget. Or let them cook dinner with you while you discuss the various ingredients and how much more the same dinner from the local takeout place would have cost.

> *Whatever a parent tells her child will help to set the behavior that child will adopt in life, at least until he or she is old enough to decide to integrate that behavior or change it.*

Heed the words of child psychologist and parent educator Haim Ginott: "Treat a child as though [s]he already is the person [s]he's capable of becoming."

Introducing the Family Conversation about Money: Six Questions

How will you teach your children about money? To get started, ask yourself these questions:

1. **What are my personal beliefs about money,** and how do they differ from the ones I was raised with?

2. **Are my personal beliefs the ones I wish my children to be raised by,** and do they require some serious consideration or behavior modification (for modeling) first?

3. **Do my partner and I have the same or similar beliefs** about money and finances? (If not, can we work to bring these belief systems closer together for the sake of our children?)

4. **Can my partner and I pledge ourselves to being true financial and life guides to our children instead of BFFs?**

5. **Am I overprotecting my children** because of my *own* fears and because I am afraid to say no?[28]

6. **Am I taking financial responsibility for my own future,** or am I (hypocritically) on my way to burdening my children one day?

---

28 Saying no is a universal challenge for parents. Numerous books (for both adults and children) are available on the topic of saying no and effective behavior modification toward that end. Google "best books about saying no," and choose one or two that appeal to you!

Expect the Unexpected: Planning for and Predicting the Unpredictable

Events crop up all during our lives that may be good, not so good, expected, and unexpected. Such events can overwhelm even the best of us and complicate our anticipated life paths.

PREPARATION: NOT ONLY FOR THE EXPECTED

For the busy women that we are, unexpected events mean that we are engrossed in our love lives, our careers, our children, and our homes—maybe all at the same time—when the bottom drops out of our lives. An unwanted career change comes out of nowhere, and our income is interrupted or drastically reduced. Or maybe we've finally hit retirement and are ready to see the world with our partner of forty years, when he or she suddenly passes away.

How can we ensure we will be OK when events such as these crop up? How can we make certain we have financial and thus life options available to us when these events arise?

We can even separate this question into two:

1. **The expected: How can we prepare for events that, over a lifetime, are likely or certain to occur:** paying for education, living on our own, getting a job, getting married, having children, retiring and creating a legacy, caring for a loved one, the eventual death of a spouse?

2. **The unexpected: How can we prepare for the events that we never imagined we would endure:** losing a job, getting a divorce, having a special-needs child, facing a financial calamity, dealing with our own healthcare crisis, the *sudden or early* death of a loved one?

The answer to these two questions is also dual:

1. We need to have conversations about these events.

2. We need to have well-constructed but flexible plans in place *that we follow.*

Let's say you banked your future on your big job and then lost it without warning. Or a love relationship or marriage goes south, leaving you in serious financial jeopardy. What if a bad business decision or an irresponsible partner means you face unimaginable losses or bankruptcy? Or your grown child *with* a child is struggling with addiction, and that means you become a mom again in your forties or fifties? You could even lose a spouse decades earlier than anyone could have foreseen. Remember the young wife and mother who lost her underinsured husband in a car accident and was forced to live with her parents and work two jobs to support herself and her children? Her aging parents had to come out of retirement to help, proving once again that the ripples from unplanned events can go on forever.

Calamities can and do happen to all of us because a lifetime is generally a long span of years, and the odds of making it through seventy or eighty years without some sort of difficulty are slim. That's the reality. But even the unforeseen can be managed with protection in place.

> **Even the unfore-seen can be managed with protection in place.**

Within these pages, we can't touch on every kind of life event, welcome or not, but we can certainly have a conversation about a most commonly unexpected event for women: divorce. Divorce is a perfect example of an unexpected event that *can* be both financially and emotionally mitigated through early, thoughtful conversation and action, years before any such event takes place. (In some cases, the conversations that take place early on can even preclude the possibility of divorce.) Either way, your work ahead of time can take a great deal of panic out of the picture, ensuring you will indeed be OK no matter what.

Still, many women feel so blindsided by unexpected events, such as the sudden disintegration of a marriage. It's not uncommon to struggle through a constellation of emotional reactions that can obstruct their ability to manage their financial well-being. The emotional roller coaster can thus narrow their options for the rest of their lives. If you or anyone you know has ever declared, "I'm so overwhelmed; I can't think about what I should do!" or conversely, "I'm sure this will all just turn out fine by itself," then heed the following.

Navigating the Emotional Roller Coaster

Are your emotions getting in the way of your ability to tackle an unexpected event? Look for these red flags so you can face them head on, seek professional assistance, and take positive action one step at a time.

Denial and Magical Thinking. Something serious has occurred, but you're still chirping along and sticking to your normal program. When friends ask if you're OK and what you plan to do, you respond that everything is fine. You reject all offers of help or referrals. Still, you have trouble sleeping at night. You may begin to make reckless decisions or revert to childlike or earlier behaviors evident during previous traumas.

Spinning. The opposite of denial. Your brain goes around in circles, coming back to the same or random questions and issues, over and over again. You have repeated conversations with friends and family about the identical issues, but they never seem to go anywhere. You ask for advice or opinions but reject whatever is offered. Your overthinking tends to go negative. You have trouble concentrating on work or daily tasks.

Awfulizing. You see your issues as one giant, overwhelming specter looming before you. You have no idea how you will be able to take on a challenge of such magnitude and so are convinced you will not prevail.

Paralysis. You can't act on any pressing issues, even though you know things are headed south. Your paralysis in that sector may creep into the rest of your life as you blow off even basic responsibilities elsewhere. You may retreat into depression or attempt to escape.

DIVORCE: THE ALL-TOO-COMMON UNEXPECTED EVENT

There's no way around it: financial issues permeate a divorce process. Will you meet such challenges with clearheaded thinking about your future, or will emotions such as denial and magical thinking get in your way?

Allyson and Ted had both been married briefly before they met (no children). Ted was thirty-five and came from a comfortable upper-middle-class background and had a good relationship with his folks. Allyson didn't have much of a relationship with her parents, who had divorced when she was young. She had been on her own since she was out of school.

Ted relied on his parents to help subsidize him as he transitioned from job to job, trying to find his calling and pay down the debt from his divorce. Ted's parents let him live in a house they owned, and, after his marriage to Allyson, the couple was allowed to reside there. Soon, Ted and Allyson were a family of four living in the house rent and property tax free. To bring in additional income, Allyson agreed to work for Ted's parents, who also provided her with a family car.

Six years into the marriage, nothing had changed except that Allyson was angry at Ted because she couldn't be home with the children full time (it reminded her of her own lonely childhood), while Ted was frustrated that he was still dependent on his folks. Ted's parents' were affected too: they were restricted by their son's inability to stand on his own. They hoped that he and his wife would soon take responsibility for their own support, yet they weren't willing to cut the cord.

Then Ted found out that Allyson was having an affair. The couple agreed to work through the rift, but when Allyson's second affair was uncovered, the marriage crumbled. When they filed for divorce, there were barely any funds to split, and the house belonged to Ted's parents, so Allyson had to relocate with limited money. Ted was hesitant to let the children live with their mother because Allyson no longer had income from his parents, and her new relationship was unstable. Ted tried to speak with Allyson about their issues, but she was highly emotional and behaving recklessly.

DON'T LET THIS HAPPEN TO YOU

Allyson ended up with no money, no home of her own, and no job. She had no relationship with her own parents and couldn't turn to them for help. Ted retained primary custody of the children because he still had a job and was living in the house that was his children's home with involved and committed grandparents nearby.

Ted and Allyson were two people who did have responsibilities to each other, their children, and Ted's overgenerous parents. Yet the couple had little in the way of a life plan, had not taken care of their separate emotional issues, and rarely considered the impact of their decisions on others. Their life choices were not made as a result of any self-examination or enlightenment or within any process other than *forfeiture*: whatever was left to them, they took.

Ted's issues were certainly many and would require sorting out with a plan for real behavioral change on everyone's part. But looking at the dissolution of the couple's marriage from the woman's side of things, Allyson fell into her choices (to embark on affairs that would probably end her marriage) without ever considering that she would also lose her means of income (her job at his parent's firm), and very probably, custody of her children. In addition, Allyson had never saved any money of her own or assessed the couple's assets, so she didn't realize that her reckless, immature choices might mean she would be left without a marriage, a job, or custody of her children. Allyson had never even looked at her monthly expenses (budget) and so had not considered how she would pay for her survival expenses, including the following:

- Moving

- An apartment or home

- A mode of transportation

- Food

- Utilities, car, and renters or homeowners insurance

- Sharing support of her children

- Legal fees

- Medical

- Clothing

Allyson lived in a state of denial. At no time in her life had she ever examined the connection between her emotional issues and her inability to build a plan for an adult life and its financial protection. While so many women wonder, "Will I be OK?" and fear becoming indigent, Allyson went through life with blinders on. Her dire circumstances didn't hit her until her divorce was final. It was only then that she thought, "What did I *do*?"

Divorce: Essential Realities

There are endless ways to look at any divorce story and the personal and financial ramifications to all involved. For your own purposes, however, it's critical to understand the following:

- You may not want to *preplan* for a divorce, but you certainly can construct a life plan that will *protect* you in the event a marriage does not survive.

- Money is not just about numbers; it is intertwined with emotions, especially during a divorce. Women need professional assistance to help them understand their emotional and financial relationships to assets such as a home, joint belongings, and furnishings. This work will help them make their best long-term decisions and not fight for the moon (or give away the farm just to move on either). That means working with a well-chosen financial advisor and perhaps a therapist, pastor, or other qualified professional.

- Negotiating a divorce requires expert financial advice before or as you work with a lawyer. When assets are divided, will you have bargaining chips? Will you unknowingly opt for the assets that are least beneficial to you, such as a house or stock portfolio that may not appreciate or be easily liquidated or a property that will be a tax burden or expensive to maintain. Work with your personal (not the family) financial advocate on these questions. For more complicated issues, you or your attorney may seek the assistance of a certified divorce financial analyst, or CDFA.

- Most women experience a drastic reduction in their standard of living after a divorce,[29] so construct a postdivorce budget to make sure you have a very clear sense of the downsizing you can expect and to aid in your negotiating process. Joint expenses will not be divided in half after a divorce; your expenses will more likely be *duplicated* even if your settlement is half of communal assets. Conducting an early, clearheaded review of options with a financial professional certified in this area can stabilize emotions and help you create a realistic plan. It can even reframe the option of divorce itself and make the prospect of marriage counseling more appealing.

- Many women neglect to think about all the little things that often won't be mentioned during settlement, alimony, or child support discussions: the children's summer camp, college, book and sports costs, extracurricular activities, dental care, and more. Incidentals add up! Don't be afraid to bring these things up, even if they end up being bargaining chips. These things *will* need to be paid for, and everything is negotiable.

- You'll need to slow down to go fast. Take the time to sideline your emotions so you can work carefully and thoughtfully through a difficult process like an adult. If there are children involved, your ex-husband will remain in your life, too, for many years to come, and how you behave during your divorce process may have long-lasting impact.

---

29   Natasha Burton, "How Women Get Screwed in Divorce," HerMoney, June 14, 2018, https://www.hermoney.com/connect/marriage/how-not-to-get-screwed-in-divorce/. On average, a woman's standard of living goes down 27 percent after divorce (a man can get a 10 percent bump).

- If you are both approaching your divorce like grown-ups, consider a *collaborative*, *mediated*, or *DIY* divorce—dramatically less expensive (and potentially less acrimonious) alternatives to conventional divorce.[30] Just make sure you thoroughly discuss your situation with your personal financial advocate first, and throughout the process, to ensure you are operating fairly but with your best interests in mind.

---

30 Jeff Landers, "The Four Divorce Alternatives," *Forbes* magazine, July 11, 2012, https://www.forbes.com/sites/jefflanders/2012/04/24/the-four-divorce-alternatives/#35674c1b20ae.

Expect the Expected: Planning for Things You Know Will Happen

Most of us hold the dream of finally retiring and enjoying life with those we love. Yet what about paying for education (for you or your children) and weddings (again, for you or your progeny)? All of these are expected and welcomed life events. Yet even the success of welcomed life events can be out of reach without thoughtful, flexible plans in place to fund such blessings and protect them throughout a lifetime.

Here again, working with a personal financial advocate to formulate plans, the earlier the better, is a solid route to ensuring the joys of your life will not be thwarted by lack of funding and protection. This is especially important because affording the life we dream about becomes more challenging each decade. Many boomers who have lived through a series of recessions are now grappling with retirement planning or management and wondering how they will manage with 401(k)s that are leaner than they had hoped. And as we've said, in our now costly society, many millennials have been forced to put off purchasing homes and cars or even starting families—things that earlier generations saw as accessible.

Whether you're focused on education or planning a wedding, are at the threshold of retirement, or are a young woman wishing you had known how to handle your twenty-first century finances better, it's not too late. And when it comes to legacy planning (yours or your mate's), if you're still here, it's still doable—as is building in protections for you should you survive your spouse. Whether anticipated events are welcomed or not, now is the time to plan for them.

Let's look at two frequently asked for examples of planning particularly daunting to women: legacy and retirement planning, and building in protections for the eventual death of a spouse.

YOUR OWN LEGACY AND RETIREMENT PLANNING

When it comes to legacy and retirement planning, women start at ages all over the map. No matter when you sit down to plan, it's important to plan *flexibly*. After all, circumstances in our lives may alter things drastically as we live on, and we simply don't know what we don't know. Where will we be living and working? Will our mate still be with us, or will we choose to be single and independent? Will our core relationships survive and thrive, or will they morph or disappear as loved ones move away or change? Will health issues or world affairs alter our lives?

While many of us worry only that we will live too generously before retirement and thus leave ourselves strapped in our senior years, financial planners routinely respond to all sorts of fears and misperceptions when one begins to work on their legacy and retirement plans.

In their twenties when they could really start to accumulate wealth and worth, many women believe they are too young to start thinking about retirement or legacy planning. In their thirties, at the birth of their first child, they know they should get started on their planning, but retirement—let alone end-of-life planning—seems so far away. Then the forties hit, and women make plans to get professional advice, but now they're caring for parents in addition to their own children (often while working hard at a career), with little time for themselves. They assume it's too late to accumulate wealth and may not know much about conserving or even optimizing assets already poised to expand worth. Saving is only one of the many tools a smart financial advocate can use to build wealth and construct conservation and protection for retirement and legacies.

Importantly, qualified advisors help create financial flexibility. They open one's mind to the vagaries of life, helping to construct plans that can bend resiliently as life changes. They can even help one to enjoy their life *more* during their retirement years while still providing security later on.

WRONG THINKING YOUR RETIREMENT

Sara and her husband, Parker, are the perfect example of a couple who weren't appropriately focused on both sides of their retirement picture: financial *and* life benefits.

Sara and Parker wanted to leave the bulk of their estate to their only child, Emma, who was still unmarried by the time they retired. Even though Emma had a good job with benefits, they lived frugally right up until retirement, denying themselves many of the things they had originally hoped to do: travel the world, buy a sailboat, move from their small condominium to a house, even entertain more frequently. At retirement, they continued to live thriftily to ensure their legacy; they figured they would scrimp on the *front* end of retirement to make sure they had enough money for themselves and for Emma on the *back* end.

But Parker passed away eight years into retirement. Sara was still healthy, and there was plenty of money to see her through her nineties. But at seventy-four, without Parker, she didn't want to travel or buy a new home by herself, not to mention sail or entertain lavishly. Sara and her husband had deprived themselves of the pleasures of their retirement "go-go" years when they still had health and energy. Even part of their "slow-go" years had lapsed while they were still scrimping. Good financial planning would have helped them enjoy careful but well-deserved distributions while still protecting them in their later "no-go" (health-challenged or more sedentary) years.

As it turned out, Emma married a wealthy widower when she was fifty, and the couple moved to Italy. They asked Sara to come live with them, but she felt that, without Parker, she was too old to start over in another culture. Sara and Parker never realized that they could have provided for Emma's future while still enjoying their pre- and postretirement years as they had dreamed.

RETIREMENT AS CAREER DO-OVER

Many of Parker and Sara's friends had also experienced unanticipated wrinkles in their retirement years. One friend, Rick, had sold his furniture business only to find out, two years into retirement, that he was bored out of his mind. Sure, he loved building furniture in his home carpentry shop, but he was running out of friends to build for. Besides, his hobby didn't bring him the excitement he had always felt running his own business and watching the profits roll in. Too bad he had closed that door behind him, he thought, when he put himself out to pasture. But with professional guidance, Rick could have looked at any number of strategies to keep his options open. Many retirees toggle back and forth between retirement and reentry into full- or part-time work, allowing their Social Security cache to grow and send them even bigger retirement paychecks when they finally put away their shingle for good.

With the help of their dream team, Sara's other friends, Ron and Kathy, used their monthly Social Security checks and IRA distributions to help them fund a small business they had talked about for years. They opened a booth in a popular home design mall nearby and spent part of most weeks wholesale shopping for beautiful home goods (their favorite pastime) that they would resell. By selling in a managed month-to-month booth instead of a store, they relieved themselves of a high-rent storefront obligation and payroll, plus they didn't have to be on site to sell or ring up. The couple could also end their commitment anytime they wanted to. Ron and Kathy's other dream was to travel internationally, buying beautiful things for the home—which they now enjoyed as a tax write-off.

Retirees also go back to school to study disciplines they had always wished they'd pursued when younger. Some find paying jobs afterward; others use their newfound expertise to consult or volunteer. And it's not uncommon for retirees to become so expert in their new areas that they launch blogs, speak at conferences or local events, or author books. One seventy-five-year-old I know of provides VIP tours of Charleston, where he was born and raised. Not only is he expert and certified; he regales his clients with fascinating stories a younger individual would never know!

Think of retirement not just as your time to relax and play but as an opportunity for your next career. What is your dream? If you can dream it, you can work with your financial advocate to make it happen.

> Think of retirement not just as your time to relax and play but as an opportunity for your next career.

RETIREMENT AND LEGACY ISSUES UNIQUE TO WOMEN

Because, statistically, women still outlive men, they ask questions such as, "If my spouse dies, how will I survive financially?" or "How can I make sure I get the care and assistance I need?" Generally, a woman does not realize that thought processes around later-life issues must be different for her when she is suddenly alone than when she was half of a couple. For instance, at the death of her partner of any gender, she will be living on *half* the Social Security she was living on when her mate was alive. Yet her expenses will *not* be halved and will probably remain just as they were: rent, mortgage, utilities, car payments, and gardening will not change. Her food costs may be somewhat reduced, but those savings are often offset by needing to hire help around the house when honey-do tasks or cleaning needs arise, by arranging for transportation that her husband may have provided if he was the only driver, and by her growing healthcare and prescription costs.

Then, too, by the time she is widowed, certain resources a woman had budgeted—even as a single individual—may be reduced due to happenstances entirely beyond her control! For instance, her IRA minimum distribution requirement may be greatly reduced because it is a percentage only of what *remains* in the retirement account. (She and her mate had already reduced that amount by drawing from it each year.) So, down the line, as she draws from the IRA account too, her monthly stipend could be cut in *half.* And what if she needs long-term or in-home care, and she did not previously purchase coverage?

These are good reasons to consider permanent life insurance and similar options early on, which can mirror the original funds both husband and wife start out with at retirement, providing a financial do-over of sorts for a spouse left alone. (Men, too, can find themselves in a "halved" situation if their deceased wives were high earners or if their marriage had been a dual-income union, although that scenario is still more likely for women left alone.) And even something as simple as delaying retirement to seventy, instead of taking it earlier, can have a very positive financial impact because unclaimed retirement benefits grow until you need them.

Start work on your anticipated life events early. Understand that certified retirement and legacy professionals are not for *other* people or only those who have already accumulated wealth. Today's woman needs not only trustworthy financial planning advice for her future security and well-being but could be well served to have a team of professionals to help guide her through life.

DEATH OR ILLNESS OF A SPOUSE

Unlike divorce, the loss of a child, or the birth of a child with lifelong health, emotional, or neurological conditions, your own and your spouse's eventual passing is an unavoidable event. Planning ahead cannot soften the pain of loss, but it certainly can mitigate ensuing financial chaos or "Will I be OK?" concerns during an already difficult time and for years afterward. As for a serious illness, we'd all like to believe we and our loved ones will never have to endure a protracted or devastating illness. Yet as humans live longer and are exposed to so many disease-contributing factors (stress, pollution, unhealthy diet, lack of exercise), our odds of escaping serious or chronic illness and passing gently from old age don't necessarily improve.

Put On Your Own Oxygen Mask First

Thinking ahead to financial implications, many people focus on paying for the cost of the immediate medical care and nursing home or in-home care. They don't always realize that with funds going first to the medical crisis, there may be little to no focus on their own needs. Especially in the event of a spouse's serious illness, the caretaking spouse will need to consider their own needs in addition to those of their partner or have no wherewithal to help her loved one or herself. Five major concerns will therefore be the following:

1. How will my ability to *work* be affected by illness?

2. How will I replace income spent on managing the illness?

3. How will I replace my mate's income lost during the illness?

4. Will I or we have enough money to live on during the medical crisis and (if I am the surviving spouse) afterward?

5. Will I be capable of calm, rational decision-making about my life during and immediately after a serious illness crisis?

How will you go about the necessary *decision-making processes* when deaths or illnesses occur? Will you be equipped for these processes as you navigate the inevitable stages of grief for the loss of a loved one or loss of health?[31] Those who have their important life systems in place and are able to be present to work through their personal issues generally survive better during a serious illness or after the loss of a loved one than do those who become frantic or untethered. Just as importantly, a partner who thinks *only* about her mate, and not about herself as well, places both of them in jeopardy. Too often, a caretaking partner burns out or becomes ill before the death of the one being cared for. It is not even uncommon for the caretaker to predecease her ill or dying mate.

> **A partner who thinks *only* about her mate, and not about herself as well, places both of them in jeopardy.**

Having conversations *now* about how you will later go about the process of making decisions can make all the difference for you and for everyone involved too. During illness or after a death, emotions will be highly charged, and people will be less likely to think clearly; they may also rush through important decisions just to be able to move forward. We are not speaking solely about financial decisions here; we are talking about *any* deliberation undertaken—even the common emotional decisions to promptly sell a home or give away all clothing and personal items immediately after the death of a spouse. Survivors often yearn for their shared home or for reminders of the

---

31 The Kübler-Ross model of the five stages of grief includes denial, anger, bargaining, depression, and acceptance. For helpful information, see David Kessler, "The Five Stages of Grief," Grief.com, https://grief.com/the-five-stages-of-grief/.

loved one later, when memories are welcome and are not bleeding wounds. Even a quick home sale strictly to free up cash may not be in your best interest, though it seems a no-brainer at the time—hence the widely held wisdom not to make a major decision within a year of a traumatic event.

DEVISING YOUR "NOW, NEXT, AND LATER" LIST

So, now is the time to talk about how your decisions, large and small, will be made. The best way to approach those decisions is to divide them into three categories:

1. What decisions have to be made **right now**?

2. Which decisions will need to be made **next**?

3. Which decisions can be made **later** (or maybe not at all)?

You and your spouse can then draw up the tick lists that work best for you under each of the three decision categories. The conversation can continue with your financial advisor, personal or family therapist, or any other qualified professional whose input may be valuable.

If married or partnered, you can divide each of your three decision areas above into two columns, one for you and one for your partner. That way, you are effectively listing what you will need to do for your partner and what you may simultaneously need to do for you. The two separate columns constitute a private conversation you are having with yourself. For instance, if your partner one day becomes terminal or dies suddenly, you will be concerned about burial arrangements for him. In his column under "Right Now," you may enter, "family members accompany me to funeral home or cemetery to make arrangements." Under your own column addressing *your* needs, you may write, "assign personal clothing needs to family friend" and "ask friend to call my home cleaning service before the after-funeral reception." These may seem like things you could handle now if you had to, but imagining what those few days might feel like will help you to realize that by delegating tasks, you will give yourself some peace and time in which you can collect yourself for the strength you will need to manage the days ahead, short and long term.

FEEDBACK, GOOD AND BAD

Asking family or good friends for feedback as you construct your list can be tremendously helpful, especially if they have been through similar circumstances with loved ones. They may ask you who's going to do the grocery shopping or wait for prescriptions while you are at home caring for an ill family member. If you are still planning to work, they may remind you that you need to keep taking time off to ferry your loved one back and forth for doctor appointments and tests. If you look to family members to assist you, you will also need to consider the widening ripple effects on them. Yet if you *don't* plan for the assistance you will need, your lack of planning will only become another's emergency.

Still, you should be advised that there is a big difference between asking others, "What am I missing here?" and "What do you think I should do?" Retaining *ownership* of your decisions is vital, for you alone will be the one living with those decisions. Moreover, not only is there is no right and wrong ways to handle illness and death, but the way you might approach such circumstances at thirty will likely be very different from the way you see them at seventy or eighty. Even the most well-meaning family and friends (including your own children) may have their own biases when they insist that it "only makes sense for you to come live with us" or that taking a month-long cruise after losing your husband to a protracted illness is "unseemly" or "self-indulgent." (How are they to comprehend that over a span of months to years, you have already worked through many stages of grief?) Often, well-meaning friends urge just the opposite—"Get out of the house, take a trip, date again"—before an individual is anywhere near ready. Friends are often anxious to see those recently widowed divest themselves of reminders such as clothing and other personal items so that the bereaved can "get on with their lives." But while to a friend, clothing is simply clothing, to the bereaved it may represent so much more.

The warning here is do only what is right for *you*, and if you do not yet know what is right for you, that entry goes under the "Do Next" or even "Do Later" heading on your list. In fact, "Do Later" can be the most essential heading, for later is often when survivors of loss first begin to move back into life, months after the last neighborly casserole has come and gone. So if later is when you would like to start thinking about sorting through your loved one's clothes, books, or papers, that's fine. And if that is when you will be ready to emerge and become social again or consider selling the homestead, that is entirely up to you, no matter how friends may urge you otherwise. Consider arranging for the burial headstone to be unveiled a year after interment. That brings friends and family together once again to remember the loved one and comfort the bereaved but also for an eminently practical and humane reason: the passing of time has lessened the shock, and the pain of loss has evolved toward learning to live without the loved one. A year after the loss, family and friends are reentering life.

ORGANIZING, NOT AWFULIZING

If you are not certain which tasks you will need to complete in your "Do Now" and "Do Next" columns after a love one dies, the internet has no end of information available to you, much of it already in the form of lists you can cherry-pick to incorporate into your own. Just google, "What to do when someone dies," and you will instantly realize that you are not alone in your inexperience.

In fact, when a serious family illness occurs or a loved one passes, just knowing your list is ready for you will provide calm in your storm. It will prevent what psychologists call *awfulizing*, or lumping your work ahead into one overwhelming, unachievable mass. Awfulizing will convince you that you are in the worst situation imaginable (which will likely result in paralysis). Researching, discussing, and organizing your decision-making processes ahead of time will ensure you (or your family members assisting you) handle only what is absolutely necessary and doable at any given time. Organizing decisions by chunking them into what you can think about now, what you can confront next, and what you will deal with later allows you to alternately conserve your strength while also augmenting your one-step-at-a-time decision-making ability. You are not forgetting or shirking important decisions; you are simply putting them in their proper place for the appropriate time.

> **When a serious family illness occurs or a loved one passes, just knowing your list is ready for you will provide calm in your storm.**

REAL-LIFE PLANNING FOR PEACE OF MIND

At fifty-eight, Julie had the decision-making conversation with her husband, Ben, sixty-two, and then with their family and personal advisors. Both she and Ben set up their lists, which were somewhat different as certain financial decisions were more important to Ben to handle earlier to give him peace of mind. Julie was more comfortable moving some of those same items until later, when she would feel better able to tackle them. But she expressed a desire to spend her final days at home rather than in a hospital, which would entail the expense of at-home care. She was concerned about Ben's well-being and her own need for dignity, so she did not want Ben to be her caregiver.

Both Ben and Julie felt that it would be important to consider their potential living arrangements early on. Ben's mother had suffered from Alzheimer's; what if Ben were to inherit the illness? They agreed that in the case of such a protracted illness, they would want to live near each other even if they could not eat and sleep together or afford long-term nursing care at home.

Their family financial planner suggested they tour local assisted living facilities to look at step-down setups. In such a facility, the couple could share an apartment, yet if one of them needed specialized care, that partner could "step down" to quarters in the nursing or Alzheimer's wing and step back up if there was improvement. The couple also discussed with their financial advisor the option of renting (instead of selling) their home, thus enabling the surviving spouse to leave the assisted living facility and return to the home, if desired.

Julie and Ben understood that facilities and even localities could change by the time they actually needed their lists, but thinking ahead about issues that were most important to them—and placing decisions in their proper place on their respective lists—turned out to be critical to the couple years later when Julie was unexpectedly diagnosed with an aggressive brain cancer. Their work on their lists— and their previous conversations with an eldercare expert accessed through their family financial advocate—allowed Ben to make certain that Julie's desire to be cared for at home by hospice (as opposed to spending her last days in a hospital) was calmly carried out.

After Julie's passing, Ben was not comfortable living alone in their home and looking after himself. Yet even with his worsening eyesight, he was still fairly active and wasn't ready to move in with his kids. The list work that he and Julie had completed paid off for him too: after a month or so with family, Ben moved to a nearby assisted living facility and relieved himself of the burden of taking care of the house, cooking for himself, and driving (which was no longer possible). The social environment was just what he needed to keep his spirits up and keep him healthy; he even played competitive bridge with friends. As he had previously discussed with his financial advocate, he rented out the family home until he was certain he did not want to return it. Then he sold it to help fund his life at the assisted living facility. A few years after he transitioned to assisted living, when Ben began to experience a series of small strokes, the step-down facility decision he and Julie had made years earlier became his perfect solution as he repeatedly moved from his own room, to the local hospital, to recovery care in his facility, and back again.

Ben and Julie's choices were made possible by their own conversations about their now, next, and later lists and via discussions with their financial advocate and expanding dream team. They also accessed advice from church and community resources. Those discussions ensured that the couple didn't find themselves boxed in without financial options to achieve or get close to their wishes—whatever those wishes looked like when they were finally needed. The discussions looked at a plan A (the ideal result) but also B and C options in the event that life didn't necessarily cooperate with plan A. Their financial advisor prompted each of them to check in with their head, their heart, and their gut and asked them, *What might possibly go wrong?* Then she suggested protections they could put in place. Ben and Julie's list preferences cut across not just health, family, and end-of-life and living arrangements but other areas as well: spirituality and their relationships with grandchildren, friends, and their communities. Over the years, both modified their list entries, for their lists were flexible. It was only important that their final wishes were just that—the decisions at which they had finally arrived.

GETTING PERSONAL WITH REALITY

In addition to working on their own lists, Ben and Julie had communicated many of their personal wishes to each other and also to their children. Thus, neither of them experienced the additional stress of family skirmishing or hostility during illness and loss. Additionally, the couple had not only completed the necessary protection and estate planning we've described earlier in this book, but they had communicated their *feelings* about how they wished to live and die and what was important to them, even if it seemed "silly."

If they hadn't been able to communicate their wishes in person, they agreed they would have written thoughtful letters or even recorded a video for their loved ones. They also made sure to complete a list of needed information for each other and their kids: important family and personal advisors; passwords;[32] location of bank accounts, insurance policies, stock certificates, and keys; subscriptions and autopayments that would need to be canceled, and so on.[33]

In effect, both Ben and Julie made clear to their children that although they might be enduring the loss of health and even life, that did not mean they were willing to relinquish their power or control over their inevitable life events. As Sheryl Sandberg and Adam Grant so eloquently put it in their best-selling book, *Option B: Facing Adversity, Building Resilience, and Finding Joy,*[34] "Option A is not available. So let's just kick the s*@$ out of Option B."

---

32   Consider password-aggregator solutions such as LastPass, Dashlane, 1Password, Keeper, and StickyPassword to streamline and secure passwords.

33   Digital options are now available to help individuals and families via online organization, storage, and timely notification to heirs of digital assets and documents. For more information, check out *everPlans*, LifeSite, Yourefolio, Afternote, AboutOne, Mustbin, Hsac, Virtual Strongbox, TDS, Keeper, and Box.

34   Sheryl Sandberg and Adam M. Grant, *Option B: Facing Adversity, Building Resilience, and Finding Joy* (London: Knopf, 2017).

Conclusion: Your Essential Takeaways

The eleven conversations about money covered in this book should provide you with valuable tools to think about adding to your arsenal. They are designed to spark a deeper look at how you think about money and what it says about you. Give yourself permission to acknowledge every emotion and concern. Acknowledge what you are thinking, feeling, and doing in the moment. Taking the time to get acutely present to what is going on is the key to evaluating your relationship to money.

Early on, we focused on what money is telling you about your values and emotions, as they act as the cornerstone of everything you do. They are unique to you; therefore, they should be authentic and specific to what you believe. If you are finding that behavior around money is not in alignment with what you feel, then you can start to make the shift and let your personal values and goals guide your money—not the other way around.

No one knows you or your relationship to money like you do, but finding the right money mentor can allow you to move faster with more focus. Acting like a Sherpa, the right money mentor can show you the path forward while providing the necessary perspective for where you have been. The key is for you to be involved and willing to be vulnerable in this undertaking.

Taking action, even if it's a small, simple step, is where you begin to create the momentum to reach your full financial potential. And if the answer or advice you are getting doesn't feel right, keep looking. Trust your gut!

Letting go of past beliefs isn't easy.

Regardless of where you are when you read this, know that your past is not as important as what you do moving forward. But when you recognize where you are being held back and how the things you learned in childhood may not be serving you today, then you gain confidence to bridge the gap between where you are now and where you want to be. By exploring the societal, familial, and personal limitations that have been holding you back from financial well-being, you now have the resources you need to take action.

Remember, financial freedom starts with recognizing what an adult relationship to money looks like and breaking ground on building the financial foundation that is right for you. But building on a foundation of sand won't work. It has to be built on a foundation of protecting your wealth in concert with growing it. Otherwise, you will always be at risk of it falling apart and feeling like you're stuck in a never-ending cycle of stress and self-doubt.

As you start to build this foundation, keep in mind that our personal relationships can affect us in ways we don't always expect. With clear thinking, we can discover communication practices that can create an environment of sharing and support. And with fresh listening, we can inquire and hear another's point of view, creating meaningful interactions that align with our values and fortify our worth.

As you gain clarity, you may notice that your plans may need to be changed. Whether it is an expected or unexpected event, life happens. Don't let fear stop you from reaching your ultimate goals, and remember that success looks different for everyone. By digging deeper to find what really matters to you, new possibilities will open up.

You will expand, grow, and evolve into a new way of thinking, ultimately giving yourself permission to claim the financial success you deserve.

FAQs

Because today's women are always ready with smart questions that cut right to the heart of any matter, let's wrap up with the most frequently asked questions women have posed about achieving their financial goals and realizing their as-yet unexplored worth.

Q. I wish I could get my financial act together, but I still don't know why I do the things I do with money.

A. Before all else, you should take some time to uncover the blind spots you have about your money. Those blind spots include emotions, beliefs, and perceptions you may have inherited from your upbringing, which may be hindering, rather than helping, you achieve your life goals and aspirations. If you want to dive into this deeper, go to www.myworthfinance.com, where there are many tools and resources to help you define your money mindset.

Q. "Finance" seems like an issue so alien to my life. Why do I need to learn about it?

A. Financial issues play a role in almost every part of our lives. In our culture, especially, there are few life events and aspects that do not intersect with the management of money. Money flows through our lives, touching everything we do.

Many women have little sense of the hundreds of weekly financial transactions they move through without realizing they are making money *decisions*. Women have the *power* to choose the dreams they wish to pursue. There are any number of choices between a year's worth of Starbucks lattes, takeout lunches, and electronic gadgetry purchases—or the once-in-a-lifetime hike up Machu Picchu or new small business launch. *Finance* is merely a word we use to describe how we *align* our money decisions with the things we say are important to us. There's no right or wrong and no rule book. Finances are unique to every adult female (or male). When women embrace their financial lives, they complete their decades-long ascent within career, life, and personal empowerment.

Q. How can we work to dispel the myth that women can't manage money?

A. Try relating this: women have always been excellent money managers when they have accepted that role. Throughout history, women have managed household and business spending practically and intelligently. In more recent times, as women's roles in the workplace and modern cultures have shifted, women have proven to be outstanding financial professionals and investors, as well. Women are by nature nurturers, and caring for others has taught them to be thoughtful, patient, and careful in their decision-making processes—attributes that are particularly well suited to investing in securities, real estate, or business. Women are also more likely to probe deeper and wait longer for better results than their male counterparts; men invest more impulsively and may be more attracted by the next shiny object.

Q. I'm too busy to deal with financial issues.

A. Nowadays, women are extremely busy people indeed. We take care of partners, children, careers, friends, extended family, and community members and often do all these things simultaneously. And women have broken through glass ceilings in so many fields: medicine, law, technology, sports, politics, and more. Yet deeply contemplating how our financial affairs influence our personal dreams and goals has been a neglected item on too many tick lists.

We are now learning that we must become *present* in our here and now or risk sacrificing our tomorrows. Women have been too prone to handle their most important, life-impacting decision-making *during* life crises instead of beforehand. This must change if we are ever to make our lives truly our own. Finding a highly qualified financial and life advocate can be an important first step. Another essential step: we must learn to "go slow to go fast" by calendaring personal retreat time in which we can creatively ponder what's genuinely important in our lives.

Can you learn to claim an afternoon, weekend, or even a nature walk away from everyone else's needs and chaos to think about what it is you want for yourself during your lifetime? If you calendar for everyone else's needs, it's time to calendar for you.

Q. You mention having a financial advocate. Why do I need one as opposed to doing this myself?

A. There are many things you can do yourself to take control of your own financial situation. Having a financial advocate will only enhance your success. A financial advocate will know current planning techniques, products, tax law, and strategies that can be instrumental to helping you plan. There is so much information out there that many find they lack the time to properly address all aspects of their financial situations. So if you want to make sure you are not missing anything or failing to take advantage of new products and features, you should seek the advice of a professional. In addition, they can tailor the advice they give you to be very specific to your values, your goals, your beliefs, and your situation. Can you do it yourself? Sure, but why not build a team of people who can partner with you to bridge that confidence gap?

Q. I wouldn't even know how to start getting my financial act together.

A. Start by gathering all your financial documents and online accounts statements. These will be essential as you need to determine where you are right now before you plan where you are going. Once you do this, categorize them based on the components discussed earlier (protection, savings, growth, cash flow, and debt). Once you do this, you should first look at your cash flow. Have you ever done a spending plan? If not, then start there. List all the things you must spend money on, the nondiscretionary items. Then list those things that you spend money on but are discretionary in nature. From there, you can start to see what you are spending money on now.

Does your spending match with your values? Does it represent the person you want to be? What is missing that would change how you feel about your situation (besides more money)? Is it a different perspective? More knowledge about particular investments? This will give you a good base for which to start a conversation with your financial advocate.

Q. Some women seem so confident about their lives; they know just what they're doing. I wish I could be that way.

A. You can! The most confident women (and men) are self-assured because *they put themselves first*. They know that, by doing so, they will be better equipped to do their jobs and take care of others. In effect, they have learned to put on their own oxygen masks first so that they don't run out of oxygen and expire before they can even help anyone else. Women can tend to be masochistic and even martyr-like in their pursuit of selflessness. But, counterintuitively, selflessness is self-defeating if it deprives you of attention to your own needs. Then it only ensures you have little left to give anyone else.

So make a choice to put on your own oxygen mask first. Then take action to fulfill and protect your life. If you're not by nature an action-oriented individual, getting present and indulging in retreat time to think about what you truly want in life will help light the fire you've needed to spur action. Working together, you and your financial advocate will set you on your road to confidence because you will know you are finally taking care of YOU.

Q. I've always been a procrastinator, so I'll probably never be able to retire. I worry that I could end up impoverished if someone else doesn't take care of me.

A. People frequently put off doing things when they fear they don't know what to do or even how to start. But you can jettison your fear of doing things you've never done before just by enlisting the help of a qualified professional. That's what expert professionals of all kinds are for, because *no one* has the time or interest to be schooled in everything they will need to know about in life. Think of the trainer at your gym or the nutritionist who is helping you learn how to eat better. These specialists need to know as much as they can to help *all* potential clients. But you only need to know *just enough* to achieve your needs and desires. It's exactly the same with money management: *you* do not have to be a financial expert—you just have to be thorough enough to locate and interview the best candidates to be your financial advocate.

Working together on your life plans, you will learn how to use "chunking," or baby steps, to make your dreams a reality. As you move through your planning and action processes, you'll learn *just what you need to know* at any juncture to achieve success.

Q. What if I can't relate to my personal financial advocate?

A. Because everyone learns differently, a well-trained financial professional cares about finding the best way to communicate effectively with you. (That includes leaving confounding financial jargon at the door.) Your advocate must be part financial pro, part life coach, part teacher, part therapist, and part emergency room "triage" doctor. The many experiences I have shared within this book should also give you a good sense of the kind of financial advocate you hope to work with. Will this person approach you gently, or regularly deliver the wake-up calls you know you so sorely need? Personalities must mesh well, and you'll want to be able to have frank discussions with the advocate you choose.

Yes, it's up to you to do your due diligence to interview and work with the best qualified individual you can find. But that individual must also be able to connect with you on a caring and genuinely interested level. If after a couple of sessions you do not feel that connection is possible, back up and continue your search for the best personal advocate possible, following the tips in the earlier conversation "In Your Corner: Finding the Right Money Mentor." Never forget that your advocate is there to help ensure your life is the one *you* envision, with all the best possible protections built in to safeguard you during life's unexpected (and expected) events to come.

Q. Can't I make a plan once and be done? Why do I have to have an ongoing relationship with my advocate?

A. Because living does not happen in a vacuum and few things in life remain static, your personal financial advocate should be by your side to step in, reevaluate, tweak your plan, and help you pivot for all of life's events, unexpected *and* expected. Understand that (1) how you see the world at twenty may have little resemblance to how you view life at forty or seventy, (2) needs and wants are constantly changing, and (3) the world changes too.

Any professional who comes to know you well becomes intimately familiar with your backstory *and* helps you design your future goals and aspirations. Therefore, he or she can proactively reach out to you to alert you to trouble ahead or to let you know it is time to meet to review previous decisions for potential shifts. Ensuring this kind of flexibility in your financial and life planning will allow you to pivot easily and maintain an agile plan, just as today's most successful and agile business enterprises do. Your financial advocate's job is to make sure that while your personal life "enterprise" operates at optimal levels in the here and now, it is always poised to move into your envisioned future too.

Q. Can't I deal with all of this sometime later? I'm not ready to give up my favorite things right now for a life later. I'm sure it will all work out eventually.

A. No one wants to be in a situation where they look back and say "would've, could've, should've." You can be fin(anci)ally free without having to make either-or decisions. You can enjoy your life now without sacrificing your safety or your dreams later; it's all about *balance.* Having said that, you must not indulge in magical thinking ("It will all work out by itself") but instead, get started setting up a powerful life plan so that you can *easily* care for it while you continue to enjoy your current life.

Q. My spouse/partner/manager/friend is handling my finances and says I should trust him/her. What's wrong with that?

A. What's wrong is that it's *your* life, *your* hard-earned money, *your* future. As an adult, you have to *make sure* it's taken care of properly, because no one else will be the loser if they neglect to do the work for you. You can certainly trust another's good intentions, but it is up to you to verify that the work is being done. Remember: You don't have to know *everything*; you just have to know *enough* to know that your future is safe. There are legions of celebrated individuals who handed over their finances and their lives to others and never checked on their money until it was too late.

So use your head, heart, *and* your gut to verify that your money is always in safe hands. Never surrender your response-ability (your own ability to respond) to whatever life has in store for you. Choose the caretakers of your freedom powerfully!

Q. I'll do my due diligence to find the best financial advocate for me. But why do I need a dream team too?

A. The intersections of your daily life and your money can be limitless. During the course of any year, those intersections may prompt the need for legal, accounting, emotional guidance, and more. Think of the *other* team members you'd have a hard time living without: hairdresser, manicurist, trainer, massage therapist, physician, gynecologist, therapist, realtor, tailor, dry cleaner, interior designer, even astrologer! And consider the team you would assemble to help you launch a business: you'd need a board of advisors representing industry expertise, finance, human resources, legal, client base, community, and more.

In the same vein, you can easily build your financial dream team because each professional in that team can help connect you to other top-flight specialists you may need. The right advocate will not only expedite such introductions for you; they routinely coordinate joint meetings to ensure that coprofessionals can weigh in on decisions that may cut across multiple areas in your life—legal and accounting, for instance. All you need to do is your due diligence in researching each individual, asking frank questions to ensure that there are no conflicts of interest or money exchanging hands. Again, verify so that you can trust.

Q. What if along the way I make mistakes?

A. Not only does everyone misstep at one time or another, but, like today's most successful enterprises, you may *need* mistakes to help you uncover new and creative options and solutions. The key is to not let the fear of making a mistake be the mistake. Procrastination is a top reason people don't engage in addressing their money issues. But not dealing with it can end up being the biggest mistake of them all. Get into action. Take small steps and go from there. Forgive yourself for missteps in the past. You can't change those. What you can change is how you move forward.

Resources

EXHIBIT 1—MEDITATION ON MONEY

Excerpted from *The Soul of Money: Transforming Your Relationship with Money and Life* by Lynne Twist.[35]

Money flows through all our lives, sometimes like a rushing river, and sometimes like a trickle. When it is flowing it can purify, cleanse, create growth, and nourish. But when it is blocked or held too long, it can grow stagnant and toxic to those withholding or hoarding it.

Like water, money is a carrier. It can carry blessed energy, possibility, and intention, or it can carry control, domination, and guilt. It can be a current or currency of love—a

35 Reprinted with permission (W. W. Norton & Company Ltd., London, 2003), republished in paperback (W. W. Norton & Company, Inc., New York, 2017).

conduit for commitment—or carrier of hurt or harm. We can be flooded with money and drown in its excess, and when we dam it up unnecessarily, we keep it out of circulation to the detriment of others.

In this condition of scarcity, money shows up not as a flow, but as an amount, something to collect and hold on to, to stockpile. We measure our self-worth by our net worth, and only and always more is better. Any drop on the balance sheet is experienced as a loss that diminishes us.

Grounded in sufficiency, money's movement in and out of our life feels natural. We can see that flow as healthy and true, and allow that movement instead of being anxious about it or hoarding. In sufficiency, we recognize and celebrate money's power for good—our power to do good with it—and we can experience fulfillment in directing the flow toward our highest ideas and commitments. When we perceive the world as one in which there is enough and we are enough to make the world work for everyone everywhere, with no one left out, our money carries that energy and generates relationships and partnerships in which everyone feels able and valued, regardless of their economic circumstances.

EXHIBIT 2—QUICK ONLINE RESOURCES FOR ADVANCE DIRECTIVES

- www.caringinfo.org (click on Advance Care Planning)

- www.aarp.org/caregiving/financial-legal/
  free-printable-advance-directives/

- www.nia.nih.gov/health/
  advance-care-planning-healthcare-directives

- www.cancer.org/treatment/finding-and-paying-for-treatment/understanding-financial-and-legal-matters/advance-directives/types-of-advance-health-care-directives.html

EXHIBIT 3—THE FOUR A'S OF INTENTIONAL DECISION-MAKING

Logic doesn't flow in until emotions move out. Until we recognize and verbalize (out loud) the emotions we are feeling, then acknowledge and affirm them, we won't be able to shed our emotional chains to respond logically to potential derailments and act in our best interest. Now that you've read this book, you have all the skills you'll need to use this exercise again and again, to keep your behavior in line with your values and ensure you stay right on track to your goals.

1. Stop and become AWARE of what you are feeling.

   - What physical sensations are you experiencing related to this decision? (Anxiety? Elation? Fear? Excitement?)

   - How are these feelings influencing your ability to think rationally? (What is your current line of thinking? What do you want to do? How are you behaving?)

   - Are others providing opinions that are triggering these emotions?

2. ACKNOWLEDGE where you are.

   - Step back and revisit your declared goals and values.

   - Have your goals changed? Have your values changed? If so, how?

- State again clearly what is important about the values you have chosen.

- State clearly how your goals connect to your values (original or modified).

- How will what you desire to do connect with these goals and values? Be specific.

3. AFFIRM or reaffirm your goals and values out loud after considering other options.

    - Is this decision in alignment with what you stated was most important to you?

    - Are there any other alternatives to consider?

    - Are you open to discussing different viewpoints?

    - What are the trade-offs and consequences to making or not making this decision? (Be honest!)

    - What is the impact of this decision on the bigger picture of your values and goals?

4. ACT knowing your choice has been an *intentional* choice and you are prepared for the outcome.

    - Based on what you have discussed with your financial advisor (per this exercise), what do you think is your best choice, given all the options?

    - State clearly the decision that is best in line with your values and goals.

    - What small action steps can you take to move yourself closer to fulfillment? List them.

- Which steps could you automate to prevent your stated goal from becoming derailed?

- How will you stay accountable to yourself to keep on track? How will you allow your financial advisor to assist you in staying on track?

About the Author

Ande Frazier, CFP®, CLU, ChFC, RICP, BFA™, ChSNC
CEO, Editor in Chief, myWorth

Ande has made it her mission to break down the emotional, behavioral, and societal barriers that stand between women and strong financial foundations.

Early in her more than twenty-five-year career, she rejected traditional planning methods that didn't account for how emotions factor into financial decision-making. Wanting to do things differently, she developed an expertise in behavioral finance.

In the years to follow, she saw again and again that conventional wisdom about women and money was flawed: it's not women's finances that determine their self-worth. It's women's sense of self-worth that determines their finances. And like that, a new philosophy was born.

In late 2018, Ande launched myWorth, a media community that's inspiring a financial awakening among women who are eager to take control of their financial journeys. She built myWorth on two core beliefs: traditional approaches to speaking to women about money are broken, and conversations about money must align directly with women's personal values and goals.

Ande rose to the top of the primarily male-dominated insurance world as the former head of a multimillion-dollar fintech company and VP at Penn Mutual. She is now widely recognized as a driving force in the financial community, holding multiple finance and insurance designations, including a CFP®, CLU, ChFC, RICP, BFA™, and ChSNC. She regularly appears on top national media outlets to speak about topics at the intersection of women and finance. She has been named one of the "Top 100 People in Finance" in 2019 and "Top 50 Women of 2019" by *Top 100 Magazine*, as well as one of Bristol's "Who's Who among Distinguished Professionals and Executives." And she received a Gold Stevie® Award for Female Executive of the Year – Consumer Services –10 or Less Employees.

Ande lives in New York and is married with two children. For more information about Ande, go to www.andefrazier.com.

Acknowledgments

There are no words that can express how grateful I am for all the people who supported me in the writing of this book, from the ideation phase to the final product. First, thank you to the myWorth team, Meredith Morris, Meghan Haley, Kate Hynson, and Kat Madamba, for reading drafts and keeping the day to day going while I was in the depths of editing. You all are rock stars who consistently rise to the occasion every day. I am honored to have all of you on my team. To Eileen McDonnell, I have learned so much from you. Thank you for encouraging me to write my thoughts and for giving me the opportunity to make such a big difference in the lives of so many women. Much love to team JJ, Jimmy Lyons and Jeff Tompkins—you both have given such wisdom and insight. I may not have liked it, but I appreciated the pushing and straight talk. So grateful to have both of you in my life. To Wimze Digital, Channel V Media, Viktoriia, and everyone on the Advantage|ForbesBooks team, thank you for nudging me and being a source of knowledge and feedback. And a special thank-you to Richard L. for his wisdom, perspective, and wordsmithing. To Vince D'Addona, for mentorship and for being one of my biggest fans. To my family, with immeasurable gratitude, my husband, Sean, who is my rock—you kept me fully supported in every way throughout this entire process. I love you. To my mother, Carolyn, for praying for me, reading drafts, and making sure my voice was being represented. To my father, Lamar, for sharing your passion and love for this business and teaching me everything you know. To my brother, Norman, for always encouraging me. And to my children, Ella and Max, for cheering me on with patience and love. My love for all of you is infinite.